THE PROJECTION PRINCIPLE

THE
PROJECTION PRINCIPLE

—

DR. GEORGE WEINBERG
AND
DIANNE ROWE

ST. MARTIN'S PRESS
NEW YORK

Design by Richard Oriolo

Library of Congress Cataloging-in-Publication Data

Weinberg, George H.
  The projection principle / by George Weinberg and Dianne Rowe.
      p. cm.
    ISBN 0-312-00057-X
    1. Social perception.   2. Projection (Psychology)
3. Interpersonal relations.   4. Self-realization.   I. Rowe, Dianne.
II.Title.
BF323.S63W45 1988
158'.2—dc19   87-38261

First Edition

10 9 8 7 6 5 4 3 2 1

ACKNOWLEDGMENTS

The authors wish to thank Brian DeFiore and Susan Rabiner, editors at St. Martin's Press, for their help with this book. Also a number of writers and professional therapists have helped a great deal at various stages. Among those whose suggestions were most pivotal were Dr. Louis Ormont, Dr. Joan Ormont, Helen McDermott, Dr. Lucinda Mermin, Margaret Scal, Dr. Henry Katz, Olivia Katz, and Dr. Hank Schenker.

CONTENTS

THE PROJECTION PRINCIPLE

1
INTRODUCTION

This book is about relationships. It will explain why some deepen and improve over time while others change for the worse. It will explain what you can do to turn an infatuation into a lifelong love affair, how you can make friendship last, and how you can develop a budding interest into a long-term career.

Your success in any relationship depends upon the way the other person sees you in his own mind—his picture of you. And you can draw that picture.

As you may have noticed, it isn't enough to be good or capable or attractive. People see you not always as you *are* but as they *think* you are.

People *project.* They attribute to you qualities, traits, motives, even an appearance that may not be yours. Because of their own psychological needs, others create an identity for you, one that suits them. Whether they unconsciously invent a picture of you, or merely exaggerate traits you already have, you are up against a Projection.

A Projection is anything a person reads into another and sees as if it were there when it is not.

There are as many kinds of Projections as there are human qualities. Someone may see you as incompetent or slow to learn. Perhaps your best friend doesn't recognize your sensitivity, or your loyalty, or the simple fact that you're grown-up and independent. Perhaps your lover doesn't see you as important in his life, or your boss doesn't see you as promotable.

Or it may be that people don't see what's best about you. If so, you may feel that you are up against a wall of opposition, and that you just can't get through to those who count most in your life.

Projections are dangerous because people who see you the wrong way will cheat you out of opportunities—in work, in love, in friendship. People treat you according to the way they see you.

If you're ever to get the things you want in the world, and be treated as you deserve, you've got to face the fact that *people do project and you must know how to deal with their Projections.* There's no sense pretending that the key is simply to make a better showing—to work harder and prove yourself. If the truth about who you are hasn't yet won out, it very likely never will, all by itself. People's Projections of you, their prejudices, won't simply go away.

But once you understand the nature of Projection, you will discover that *you have control over how people see you.*

The Projection Principle will give you a whole new way of thinking about relationships. It will give you a tool for shaping the way other people see you. You can stop them from forming wrong impressions of you and keep them thinking highly of you. Even if someone is biased and ready to see you at your worst, or if his opinion of you has started going down, your ultimate worth to that person is *still up to you.*

Use of the Projection Principle can often save love relationships. For example, most failures of love occur through gradual loss, though the rupture may come abruptly. The other person begins to *see* you as somewhat less magical and vital. Sensing some change, you try harder. Long before the person says, "I like you but you are not the one for me," you knew that day was coming. You perceived tiny signs of its approach, and now it is here.

When you lose out on a love affair, or a job, or any relationship through another person's failure to see the real you, you may be tempted to say, "That's *his* problem," and just carry on. But to do so would be to ignore the sense that you could have done something to come across as you wanted to. And not by dressing better, or improving your vocabulary, or being sharper in any way.

You could have used the Projection Principle to make that person *hear what you were really saying and see who you really are.*

When you feel that you're not getting through to someone you love, or that others without your talent are being favored over you, you don't have to sit by idly. There is much you can do to affect the way a boss, a lover, a friend, a fellow worker sees you. You are not locked into their perceptions. Their prejudice is not *their* problem alone. It is *your* problem. How they see you and how they treat you ultimately is in your hands.

Psychologists have taught us that a person's usual ways of seeing others develop in childhood, and this is so. The man who thinks women are stupid, or are there only to serve him, or are out to take him for all his money—in almost every case, learned early in life to see women that way. His way of perceiving is a habit—a habit of mind.

But psychologists have also implied that there's nothing you can do to alter the way people see you. A woman, whose husband admired her before they were married, realizes that he's starting to distrust her; he has begun to make accusatory statements and to question her about things she's told him. Back in his college days, he eloped with his first wife but grew so relentlessly suspicious of her that their relationship became impossible. Now his wife sees the same thing happening with her. Psychologists have said in no uncertain terms that in such a case the man's true way of perceiving women is coming out and that such a woman can only watch helplessly as her status declines. They have not realized that the woman, on her own, can teach her husband to trust her and convince him that she loves him faithfully.

The message of psychology has been loud and clear: If someone doesn't see you for who you are and treats you poorly on the basis of his misperception, there's nothing you can really do to get better treatment.

However, *The Projection Principle* is a stunning new concept that you can use to induce people to see you as you are.

You can also use the principle to stop *yourself* from projecting, and to read other people correctly.

Your own Projections can be as dangerous to your happiness as those of others. You may be losing out because you're fearful and see the world as dangerous, or because everyone seems to disappoint you, to let you down. You may misjudge people and make repeated mistakes in relationships, or be jealous of those younger or older than you. Or you're unhappy and see other people as more independent, more capable, more vital than you—so you settle for a second-class job or a mediocre lover. Everyone seems way ahead of you. Friends try to encourage you, but your picture of the world just doesn't let you move. In such cases, it is *your picture of others* that has to be changed.

Using a straightforward process, once you know it, you can alter the way others see you, even if they don't realize that they're projecting. And you can eliminate flaws in your own outlook that keep you from seeing others as they are.

Our technique for clearing up other people's perceptions doesn't demand that you sit for hours using complicated strategies to talk the person out of his wrong view. Nor does it require you to know anything about psychotherapy beyond what we're about to tell you.

Once you train yourself to spot Projections and understand what sets them in motion, you can attack them in other people and in yourself. You can break in on the process and induce other people to stop distorting, *more often than not, without the other person's even knowing what you did.*

And you can also teach yourself to see others differently, to keep your exuberance about life, ending your own Projections and improving such relationships.

When you understand the Projection Principle you will see that you can apply it almost everywhere—in love relationships, in long-term relationships with friends, family, business associates, and with the next-door neighbor. *You can assert a steady influence over how these people see you.*

Almost as important, you can use it with individuals you don't like and whom you would never seek out unless you had to. We've all had to deal with an unfair teacher or a bad boss or an obstreperous neighbor. Although we may never expect to have such people as friends, our livelihood or our peace of mind may depend on our ability to handle these relationships.

In fact, you can even apply the Projection Principle in

very short-term relationships, such as those with a doctor treating your illness or a cab driver taking you to the airport.

Remember, it isn't enough to be good or fair or kind if you're constantly misunderstood or underestimated.

What we're about to ask you to do may seem radical at first. But you're going to use a truth hardly ever expressed and yet profoundly important: How a person treats you doesn't only *reflect* his picture of you. It *forms* it.

2

WHAT IS
THE PROJECTION
PRINCIPLE?

—

Suppose you knew exactly how others saw you. You could stay away from an acquaintance who thought of you as a pushover. You might avoid someone who saw you only as a sex partner and nothing more, and favor someone who saw you as worth building a life with.

You'd know when a relationship was a dead end, so you could escape the anguish of trying to get through to an impossible person, who saw you as stupid, hysterical, or oversensitive. You might refuse to work for a boss who didn't see you as promotable.

Ordinarily, we don't pause one second to ask ourselves what a person thinks of us or how he sees us. Does my daughter consider me a prude? Does my best friend realize that I'm loyal, that I have her interests at heart? Does my husband rely on me the way he should?

But the instant things go wrong in a relationship, a hundred questions of just this kind—"What does this person think of me?"—flash into our minds. "Am I at fault or does he have some false picture of me?"

Ellen's husband, Steve, has gradually stopped confiding in her about his work. Does he see her as uninterested? If so, did *she* do something that turned him off, or has he come to feel that she's not bright enough to offer anything helpful? Or even worse, maybe he's decided that she gives *bad* advice.

As Ellen slowly realizes that Steve no longer turns to her about his business, she goes from effortless interaction to a state of alarm. She lies awake nights wondering what she looks like to Steve, searching for clues in every little detail of the previous day.

WHEN TO USE
THE PROJECTION PRINCIPLE
———

Caution: Sometimes the other person, (in this case, Ellen's husband, Steve) is justified in his view. To find out, you should think in terms of asking him certain questions:

1. *Why the new behavior toward me?* ("Why have you stopped confiding in me, Steve? Do you see me as uninterested in your work?")

2. If you hear the worst, undaunted, you must ask him why he holds that opinion of you and get examples. *What have I done to deserve it?* Under no conditions, defend yourself,

even if you think he's dead wrong. It's vital to get the information.

(Maybe at first Ellen will think her husband is over-reacting and will feel herself getting furious or collapsing. But after hearing him out and thinking things over, maybe she'll realize he's right. Perhaps Ellen cut Steve off or often yawned or did other things while Steve talked about his work, which made him think she was bored. He is seeing her *as she has actually been*—uninterested.) There is no Projection at work.

That's the easy version. The other person will be relieved to get things off his chest.

3. Go to work on changing yourself right away. And ask the other person to tell when you lapse into your old ways. *Caution: If everyone sees something about you, it's probably true.* People have been telling Sarah that she looks grim and self-absorbed, and they're not inviting her places the way they used to. Now, she's sitting in a restaurant with two friends and the waitress jokingly asks them, "Is your friend always so glum?"

In such a case, it's got to be Sarah. Who else could it be? The world hasn't teamed up in a conspiracy against her.

If you were in Sarah's position, this is what you could do.

Step 1: Ask the friends at the table if you *are* that way.

Step 2: Assuming they say that you are, tell them you're sorry. That won't hurt. Once again, there's no Projection. *You actually are the way they see you.* Changing will be up to you.

Step 3: Look for clues as to when you're acting grim and self-absorbed. You may notice that you're worse when you indulge certain lugubrious thoughts: about your trouble at work, about the rent going up.

Even before you start dealing with the depression in your

own way, you can stop inflicting the symptoms on all your friends. Losing people close to you will only make things worse.

AXIOM I: If a particular person is treating you badly because he sees you as defaulting, your first move should be to determine if he's right.

If he's right, you don't need the Projection Principle. You need to amend your behavior.

AXIOM II: If everyone says you're short-tempered, selfish, pedantic, or whatever, then the majority is probably correct. You don't need the Principle, you need to change.

The Projection Principle is for people who are misperceived, who are paying a price or losing out because others don't see them as they are. It is for anyone who is the victim of a distortion.

A Projection is anything a person reads into another and sees as if it were there when it is not.

A Projection is always something that a person imports to the reality. What he thinks he's seeing on the screen in front of him is at least partially what *he* put there.

Let's say that when Ellen asks Steve why he's stopped confiding in her about his work, he has no real answer. All he can muster are a few loose statements about women not understanding the business world.

Years ago, Steve used to direct such aspersions toward his first wife and some women in his office. But he always made it clear that he was proud of Ellen: She was different. When they got married, Ellen was vice-president of a prominent advertising agency, and Steve considered her an exception to his rule.

Over the last five years, however, Steve has apparently

demoted her in his own mind, little by little. Looking at things now, the facts seem unmistakable to Ellen. In the beginning, he would often invite her to lunches with his clients. And even when he couldn't, or she couldn't make it, he would give her a detailed rundown afterwards and ask her for her opinions. Not only did he often take her advice, he would tell her later what a crucial difference it had made.

But his invitations stopped after a year, and the following year she quit her job to have a baby. He had given her superficial reasons for leaving her out of things—the clients didn't want extra people along—and she had let it go. He still discussed his work problems with her though, when he came home in the evenings. The two of them would often stay up late at night together going over campaigns. There was real romance in that. Then, last year, that stopped too.

More recently, Steve took to making snide comments about Ellen's old job. The agency she worked for handled inferior accounts, he would say; they traded in volume not quality, and the people were second-rate. He once even called her a token woman executive there.

One thing was certain. He had come to see her very differently from the way he did at the start of their relationship. Now Steve's Projection on Ellen is that she is "scattered and incompetent like all women."

It often occurs, as in this case, that the way a person sees you changes for the worse over time, and not because you did anything to merit the demotion. The person saw you accurately at first, but gradually diminished you in his own eyes.

You need the Projection Principle.

In other cases, a person has *always* had a wrong picture of you, and you've been unable to correct it.

Marilyn's mother sees her as socially inept and unable to relate with people, and always gives her advice.

When Marilyn was little, her mother told her exactly what to say when she was taken to visit a relative. Before Marilyn could get the words out, her mother would say, "Thank your aunt for the dinner, dear." In adolescence, her mother briefed her before every date and debriefed her afterwards. She insisted that Marilyn take dancing lessons "because she has no natural grace."

Now, at twenty-eight, Marilyn has numerous friends and a lover, none of whom sees her as awkward. She's a highly social person and well-liked.

But she hates going to dinner at her mother's because her mother *still* talks to her as if she were in danger of being dropped out of the human race. When Marilyn mentions anyone in her life, her mother asks if that person likes her and how she treats them. Her mother seems surprised to hear that Marilyn gets along with people.

Marilyn's mother is locked into a perception of her that *has nothing to do with her and never did.* Marilyn may have believed her mother in the early years, but now it hurts to have her mother see her this way, and it creates a distance between them.

In this kind of case, the person has *always misperceived you,* underestimated your worth and your abilities. As Marilyn did, you will have to make use of the Projection Principle if you are to set things right.

To sum up, in the first case, Ellen's husband *developed* the insulting Projection that his wife was incompetent in business affairs, and generally.

In the second case, Marilyn's mother simply *maintained* a Projection she *always* had—that Marilyn was insensitive and socially awkward.

AXIOM III: You need the Projection Principle if someone is projecting on you a trait you don't have, with harmful effects.

It could be a long-standing Projection of his or a developing one.

In our last case, *the Projection is your own.*

Martin sees every woman as out to exploit him emotionally and financially. His father had deeply loved his mother, even though she had been unfaithful and made a fool of him, and Martin doesn't want to be in the same spot. He wants sex without affection because affection could unman him. He's guarded about what he spends, about showing tenderness, and he responds badly when a woman takes his hand in the street. He wants a relationship, and yet he doesn't want one. He projects onto all women "a conniving mentality" that would make it seem a grievous error for him to fall in love.

When, in spite of himself, Martin does find himself in love, the woman, in response to his indecisiveness and withholding, eventually gives up on him. In a heated argument, she tells him how she pictures him as seeing her. Alone and mulling over his defeat, Martin becomes aware of a pattern in the way he sees women and wants to do something about it.

Martin needs to use the Projection Principle if he is ever to form a happy and lasting relationship.

AXIOM IV: You need the Projection Principle if you are regularly projecting on another person or a group of people, with harmful effects.

FOR BETTER
OR FOR WORSE

Not all Projections will get you in trouble. Romantic love, pity, humanity, compassion, forgiveness, mercy—these are qualities we project on the universe that enhance our lives and heighten our experience. These Projections don't *contradict* reality (they are not lies). They are simply ways of *experiencing* reality.

Two homely people fall in love and see each other as beautiful. They are both enriched. A schoolteacher sees all students as worthy. She is better off than the teacher who coldly evaluates which children are worth her time. The former delights in her whole day, and the latter does not.

It's okay that love is blind as long as it's mutual. You don't need the Projection Principle if your relationship is working.

However, sometimes what seems like a rosy projection, favorable to all concerned, can be devastating. This can happen if the favorable Projection is based on the denial of a truth, or if it amounts to an obsession about one part of a person excluding the rest of him, or if it is so lofty that it results in expectations that cannot be met.

The man who trusts all beautiful women may marry someone who doesn't love him. He's so overwhelmed with her appearance that he's incapable of seeing her scorn for him. His Projection is that "Beauty on the outside means beauty on the inside." When she's unresponsive or critical, he simply sees her as superior and feels unworthy of her. When she ridicules him in front of friends, he attributes it to her sense of humor and begins to see himself as a joke.

In another case, a man with a similar idolatry of pretty

women has found such a woman who really loves him. But he destroys her love by his fixation on her beauty. He inhibits her from expressing her earthier side, and he looks disappointed when she's less than perfect.

His constant references to how gorgeous she is unnerves her, and she understandably wonders how he'll feel about her in ten years. His Projection of her as "a glorious young beauty" makes *her* life miserable. Meanwhile, the man senses that she's more comfortable with others than with him, and he can't understand why.

These Projections pose as favorable, but they aren't as terrific as they seem. The man who trusts *all* beautiful women and marries one who doesn't love him may be oblivious to her disdain. On the other hand, a man who marries a beautiful woman who *does* love him, if he focuses only on her beauty, is likewise unable to appreciate the whole person. In each case, the Projection cheats the man out of a full experience, and in the second case it also cheats the woman. Because these "favorable" Projections aren't leading to happy relationships, they need to be dispelled.

AXIOM V: Many Projections that pose as favorable create distance and alienate.

WHAT ARE
PROJECTIONS MADE OF?

The key to controlling Projections is to know what they are made of.

Common sense tells us that people treat us as they see us. It also seems to follow that if we want someone to treat us better, the only way to achieve this is to prevail upon him to see us differently.

But how can we do this?

Psychoanalysis has told us that a person's way of seeing others starts in childhood and becomes frozen, as if a mold was formed back then. Analysts say that everyone reaches back into his or her childhood for images to represent new people who come along. Each person has a "representational map" from which they draw and which is timeless and set.

If this were so, Martin would be doomed to always picture women as betrayers of men. No matter how loyal a woman was to him, she would be unable to convince him that she was an exception, that she was really trustworthy.

If psychoanalysis were correct about Martin—that his "mode of perception" decides everything and that this mode was set in childhood—then nothing short of psychoanalytic treatment itself could loosen the mold. No woman alone could possibly get Martin to see her as she really is and treat her with the respect she deserves.

In short, if another person's way of seeing us is *invariant and if it dictates the way he treats us,* there would be nothing we could do to get the person to see us as we really are and treat us accordingly.

But we *have* a way.

The crucial concept is that the relationship between how a person sees us and how he acts toward us works both ways. *How people treat us affects the way they see us.*

If Martin can be prevailed upon to take a chance on a woman—to express emotion, to trust her with secrets, to share ideas with her, to spend money on her, to remember her birthday, to say he misses her when he does, even to say "I love you"—*he will after a while change his vision of her.* She will look to him like the first woman he's ever met that he can truly trust and love.

Actually, if Martin has even a small hint of those feelings, his converting them into actions will enlarge them. What we nourish within ourselves grows.

Admittedly, if he had *no inkling* of those feelings, then even performing those actions wouldn't help. It's not a matter of manipulating people into action. It's a matter of getting them *to heighten the faintest glimmering of a viewpoint— of a new perception of us.*

Everyone has the seeds of almost every perception inside of them. Given encouragement, people can act in ways that form almost any kind of perception.

Actions create whatever projections we hold.

If we get someone to treat us as we want, that person will see us as we want to be seen—not at once, but after a while.

AXIOM VI: Everything we do involving another person has an effect on our own view of that person. Our acts etch in our own mind a picture of the person, reinforcing the view of him that motivated those acts.

For example, if in a moment of fondness, after a long day at the office, you drive several miles out of your way to pick up the latest issue of your husband's favorite magazine, you are reinforcing in your own mind how much you love him. The act stamps in and enlarges the feeling you had, the picture of your husband as precious, that motivated the action.

The reason a person ordinarily stays the same in his Projections is that after forming a picture early in his life *he continues to act in ways that reinforce it.* Without knowing it, he is *reproducing* his representational map over and over again.

AXIOM VII: Actions sustain and reinforce Projections.

FESTINGER'S
LAW OF CONSONANCE

People have a need to stay consistent in their lives, to follow what the psychologist Leon Festinger called "The Law of Consonance." So if someone decides you're stupid and perceives you that way, he'll talk down to you and exclude you in a variety of ways. For example, if a boss has a picture in his mind of you as "low level," it may be necessary for you to get him to change more than one kind of behavior.

But the Law of Consonance works in your favor, too. Once the boss stops sending you out for coffee and leaving you out of meetings, he will on his own improve his treatment of you in other ways. People have a strong need to see themselves as logical and consistent in what they do and think. It's uncomfortable for someone to feel that he has been wrong, or acting erratically, and so the tendency is to find evidence in favor of what one already believes and to justify what one has already been doing.

In the simplest application of consonance, a person will tend to find further bad things about someone he has already mistreated, and to find additional good things about someone he's treated well.

In the case of the boss who sends you on errands and excludes you from conferences, the Law of Consonance is operating in two ways. First, it is disposing the boss to add other downgrading actions to those he already engages in. Doubtless, some of these are going on behind your back. He may disparage you to your colleagues, or merely smile if your name is put forward for a plum assignment. He may automatically leave your name off the Christmas merit bonus list. Second, the boss's need to be logical makes him *see* you as a loser. You *must* be if he's treating you this way!

But, when you get the boss to change *some* of his insulting behaviors, that same Law of Consonance will induce him to change *other* such behaviors. Staying consistent, soon he'll automatically nod agreement when someone speaks well of you. He'll begin thinking of you as a potential winner as he acts consonantly with his new behaviors.

AXIOM VIII: People's need for consonance and desire to avoid "dissonance" implies that once people start adopting behavior of any kind, they will seek other behavior consistent with it.

When you hate someone, you tend to deal with him "consistently" and overlook all his virtues: you even discount evidence suggesting that he has some decent traits. This is the flip side of the observation that love is blind.

THE
PROJECTION PRINCIPLE
—

The Projection Principle is the application of these truths. It tells us that:

If you can get a person to stop acting in accordance with a wrong perception and to treat you in a new and desired way, the person will, after a while, see you in the new way. He will then find a variety of other desired ways of acting that are consonant with his new view of you. These will further reinforce his new, good Projection.

The Projection Principle will dissipate lifelong Projections and stop harmful Projections from forming. You can use it on yourself and on others.

The purpose of this book is to show you how to use the Projection Principle for two purposes:

1. *to keep others seeing you as you really are,* and
2. *to teach yourself to read others correctly.*

We'll be developing these two methods throughout the book, showing you how to spot Projections—your own and other people's—and change them. Let's outline the steps here.

CHANGING ANOTHER PERSON'S PROJECTION: STEP-BY-STEP

Changing other people's views of you is a seven-step process.

1. You identify a Projection. A person sees you in some untrue and uncomplimentary way and is treating you accordingly.
2. You intervene in order to stop the bad treatment.
3. The other person will have one of several reactions. He may understand your complaint immediately and treat you as you want him to.
   Or
   He may start to treat you as you ask but feel that you're being uppity or demanding or oversensitive. Accept that. The important thing at this stage is that *you get him to change the behavior,* not that you get him to change his mind!
   Or
   He may refuse to heed you and refuse to treat you differently. This suggests the beginning of the end, though you may wish to try again.
4. You may have felt uncomfortable confronting him, and he may initially feel uncomfortable *being confronted* and now having to treat you differently. This is a stage you must survive.

5. As he continues to treat you in the new way, he will gradually start seeing you as you want him to. He is no longer reinforcing his old negative view of you (as incompetent, unloving, and so on) but is enlarging whatever favorable view of you he held.

6. As he continues treating you in the new way, he will start adding other positive acts consonant with his improving view of you. You may not even see these. For instance, he may speak well of you to others or stop taking precautions against you—such as withholding information—that you didn't even know about.

7. Finally, after repetition of his new way of acting toward you, his whole new view of you will be comfortable to him: it will feel natural. The Projection Principle will have changed his view of you from bad to good. He will see you as you are at best.

Let's consider briefly what Ellen might do to regain status in Steve's eyes.

1. She must identify how he's treating her and his loss of belief in her.

2. She must *intervene.* First, she might ask more questions about his work. "Exactly what happened at the meeting this morning? What's your strategy?" In addition, she must object when he disparages her own abilities or those of other business women.

3. If there's no change, she must become adamant and state the problem more explicitly. At this point, let's say Steve reluctantly confides in her but sees her as oversensitive.

4. During this period, she must endure the distress that arises from having confronted Steve and of his feeling that he can't please her and that she's uppity and difficult.

5. Now that Steve is treating her better and not reinforcing his disdain, he's beginning to remember how much he valued her advice in the past.

6. Following the axiom of consonance, he treats her more respectfully in other ways, telling his partners that a slogan was "Ellen's idea," picking up a new business book on the best-seller list for her birthday.
7. She's in good standing again. Steve's disparaging Projection has been stopped dead, and soon he won't remember ever excluding her.

CHANGING YOUR OWN PROJECTION: STEP-BY-STEP

——

For you to change your view of another person or group of people, the sequence is simpler:

1. Identify the Projection itself. (For example, you worry that almost everyone is better educated than you are and that people look down on you.)
2. Determine at least some of the actions that you engage in *because* of the Projection. (For instance, keeping your opinions to yourself, or never asking questions so you don't look stupid.) Realize that they are reinforcing it.
3. Categorize the behavior into acts that you consider easy to change, versus those you think will be hard to change.
4. Make the easier changes first, enduring the discomfort. (Force yourself to ask a friend to explain the problem with your car.)
5. As your picture of the other person and those like him changes, you will find it easier to change the rest of the behavior you've discovered.
6. Finally, you will feel natural perceiving the person or persons in a new way and acting accordingly. (There's plenty that other people don't know too!)

This time, let's look at Martin's case.

Having broken up with a woman and been criticized, Martin realizes how unfair he's been to her and to himself. Similar comments from former lovers ring in his ears. Now, he's starting a new relationship and wants to change his Projection and give this love affair a chance.

1. He determines a list of actions that he engages in routinely because of the Projection. He realizes how he's reinforcing his distance from women by stifling any urge to communicate affection to a woman or to be generous.
2. He decides that the easiest thing for him to do first would be to stop complaining about money and plan to spend a little more on the woman. He begins bringing her flowers, buying better wine for dinner, and picking up small items for her apartment.
3. It's much harder for him to call apropos of nothing and say "I miss you." But he forces himself to do that, too.
4. Gradually, he starts to enjoy expressing affection. He delights in the woman's genuine pleasure at small things and starts adding more details to his courtship of her. Making her happy becomes a basic part of his life.
5. He's closer to her than he's ever been to a woman before. She seems to him appreciative and loyal, the first woman in his life who's really on his side.

Conclusion:
New Actions → Tentative New Projections → More New Actions → Natural New Outlook.

SUMMARY

We have observed that when people see others unrealistically—unfavorably and sometimes even favorably—serious harm can come to relationships. Such distortions are Projections.

Any Projection, whether old or just developing, is accompanied by *actions* consistent with it. These actions arise from the Projection and keep it going in the mind of the person who projects.

If you *intervene*—that is, get the person to stop the actions that go with the Projection—you will, in effect, starve it and cut off its life. Once the person stops the actions that reinforce his old picture of you and substitutes actions of a new and better kind, he will see you differently and nurture a new Projection.

The way people see you is a habit of mind that depends on how they treat you. You can get them to change that habit of mind by prevailing upon them to treat you differently. And you can change your own ways of perceiving others by new ways of acting towards them.

It is *your* responsibility to keep up your worth in the eyes of those you choose in your life. It also incumbent upon you to keep *yourself* seeing people realistically and optimistically.

But how can you recognize a Projection?

3

HOW CAN YOU
TELL WHEN SOMEONE
IS PROJECTING
ON YOU?

Any untruth in our lives will generally come back to haunt us. This may not seem so obvious when we lie for a "good" reason—to make our spouse feel better about himself or to cover up a mistake we made at the office. The short-term gains are very clear. But if we back ourselves into a corner of telling our husband that he's writing the "great American novel" when we really think it's inferior, or of blaming our failure to write a letter on the mail room that supposedly lost it, we find ourselves dreading the repercussions. Even beyond that, we dull our own sense of good and bad, of truth versus untruth. We inevitably begin to lose touch with what we really feel.

Virtually every lie is injurious because of its fallout.

Projections are lies the other person tells about us. They are lies the person sustains. Whether seemingly favorable or unfavorable, as the person acts upon these lies, they tend to grow in his mind, erasing in time any possibility of a real picture of us.

To spot a Projection is to spot an untruth about us. It makes no difference whether the person *knows* he's telling himself this untruth or not. He is in a pattern of constant self-persuasion, "acting" himself into believing that we are someone we are not.

EARLY
WARNING SYSTEMS
—

Because Projections cannot remain static but must grow and become larger, it's much easier for you to nip a Projection *early,* rather than later, when it is firmly established.

The time may come when you simply won't have the resources to stop the person at all. He will become so *sure* of who you are—that is, of his *wrong* picture of who you are—that you won't be able to discourage him or convince him of the truth.

Cynthia's lover has turned her into his mother because she handles things so well. At the start of their relationship, Cynthia did everything she could think of for Howard in an effort to win his love. He wasn't a natural giver, but she thought he might learn from her example and be moved to respond in kind. But the opposite has occurred. Howard's Projection on Cynthia is that she can and should handle everything to do with his comfort, regardless of her own needs, physical condition, or other obligations.

Now, she's saying to herself, "I was a moron to try this

technique. It was stupid and dopey and self-destructive and women have been doing this to themselves for years. Even Simone de Beauvoir can't help me now." And she's probably right.

Cynthia missed a dozen chances to intervene without going berserk: she could have told Howard to pick up his own laundry one weekend, she could have suggested *he* stop at the grocer's one night a week. From the beginning, she was aware in some part of her mind that far from turning into a giver like her, Howard was making himself more and more of an infant, depending on her to be his mother.

If Cynthia tried to intervene now, after two years, since she is Howard's "mother," she'd only look like a nag. Her only choice is to come across as either "good mother" or "nagging mother." Howard can't even hear the woman who was once his lover. She's lost to him forever behind the mask of mother.

AXIOM IX: It is crucial to spot early warning signs of a Projection in the making. Denying its to yourself amounts to joining in with the lie.

There's an unfortunate paradox here. The signs are easiest to spot when the Projection is hardest to break. In the beginning, when a Projection is simpler to overturn, the signs are very subtle. Later, they are amplified as the Projection takes on a life of its own. By the time you can no longer even think of denying the signs, the Projection may be impossible to stop.

A woman feels a slight strain with a man on their first date. He recommends the entree and the wine in a way that makes it hard to contest his preferences. He delivers the woman's order to the waiter, implying that she should not speak to him. At home after the date, the woman feels somehow unsettled, though the man's decisiveness contrasts well with the wishy-washiness of the person she just broke up with.

On their next date, it's more of the same, but she also notices that the man takes her arm crossing the street in a way that makes her feel like an invalid. "Maybe it's me," she tells herself. "I'm not used to a real man."

If the relationship continues and the woman goes on trying to erase the recognition of her own discomfort at being treated like a frail child, she's headed for big trouble. By the time the man gets to the point of giving unmistakable signals—asking her to quit her job because "You meet the wrong kind of person there" or telling her not to drive in the rain—it would be extremely hard to make him hear her and reconsider his Projection of her as "delicate and needing protection." He would perceive her as a whining ingrate.

In other cases, it may be tempting to dismiss early warning signals because things seem acceptable now. But they're going to get worse. The consequences of not facing up to a Projection can be disastrous.

For instance, we would be terribly upset if we heard a teenage girl say, "I don't care *why* he stays with me—sex, whatever—as long as he *stays,* as long as he marries me!" We might be tempted to reply that five years from now, when he leaves her for someone he's *really* in love with, she'll wish she had faced his actual view of her as a "sexual convenience" earlier and had children with someone else.

The treatment that accompanies any Projection spreads like a malignancy as the Projection grows.

The boss may start by sending you out for coffee. He then adds other actions that slight you as his Projection of you as "low level and dispensable" continues to grow: he forgets to inform you of his decisions, he leaves you out of meetings and lunches, he doesn't introduce you to a visiting customer. Soon, it's natural for him to pass you by for promotion and favor a newcomer over you. By the time a budget-cut forces him to ax one person, he doesn't have to think twice—in fact, he doesn't have to think at all before sending you on your way.

AXIOM X: Once a Projection starts, it grows because the person projecting begins adding new actions based on what he already believes about you. The bad treatment spreads and worsens. The person continues to add behavior consonant with what he's already doing.

This is why it's crucial to attack Projections early and relentlessly. Hence, the enormous importance of spotting early warning signs.

WATCH FOR THE FLARES: THE SIGNALS THEMSELVES

Your own emotional responses are the best instruments you have. Your own feelings are the best indicators of what others are doing to you. A vague sense of imbalance, the impression that someone isn't hearing you or is saying yes for the wrong reasons, a hazy feeling of ambiguity that causes you to spend time puzzling out someone's meaning after a conversation—these may be the first rumblings you experience of another person's Projection in the making.

It is in this first stage that you are most likely to try to deny that there is anything wrong, especially if you love the person or if he is important in your life. But remember, that would be the worst thing for the relationship.

The right thing to do is to face the possibility of a Projection and go on the alert for *specific signals.* With a true Projection, you will usually find several or more of the following indicators appearing simultaneously, and there will be repeated incidents of them:

1. *The "not me" feeling*

Bill, an industrial researcher, is a brilliant mathematician. He's also extremely kind, loving, and sensitive to others. He's interested in cooking, design, photography, and a number of other things and considers math to be an important part of his repertoire—something he's excelled at since childhood, but far from his whole life. He meets and falls in love with Susan, an aspiring fashion writer, and has fantasies of spending his life with her. They have wonderful times together, but something feels wrong. Bill has the vague feeling that Susan doesn't really know who he is. As a mathematician would, he investigates the problem as dispassionately as he can. He remembers that the previous night she called him a "genius" three times. She regaled friends with a story of how bad *she* had always been at math and how stunning his expertise is. She's recently taken to saying, "You can solve anything, there's nothing you can't figure out with your math."

But Bill doesn't feel like a solitary genius. He feels like someone on the outside looking in as Susan admires an exalted figure that she's created. *He,* Bill, wants to be Susan's lover, but her Projection on him as "lofty genius" gets in the way. There's so much of him she's not seeing at all.

Often one of the first flares we can identify is what psychologist Hank Schenker calls the "not me" feeling. We get a sense that what the person likes about us *is not truly us,* but some idealized version of us, or an exaggeration of some part of us. It may be our best part—competence, worldliness—but the person seemingly won't accept us as being less than ideal in these respects. When we blunder or show ignorance and turn to him for help or even sympathy, he becomes suddenly blind to us. It's as if we don't exist except in the ideal.

Gradually, as we study the relationship, it becomes clearer that we've been slotted for a particular role. At first, we may take it as a compliment, especially if it's new for us. The person mistakenly views us as having everything, as needing nothing.

2. *Typecasting*

Along with the "not me" feeling, we often have a sense that we're being typecast. The person sees us not as an individual but as a typical member of some group that he either likes or dislikes.

Tom resents growing older and wants relationships only with younger women. Erica goes out with him because he's interesting, but after a short time she realizes that he's overwhelmed by a single trait of hers—namely, her youth. Tom's Projection of her is that of "younger woman interested in me." Most of what Tom seems to like about her would hold for *anyone* her age. He tells Erica how smooth her skin is, he comments on the fact that she doesn't need glasses or as much sleep as he does. Also, he continually refers to himself as being old, so she knows age is always on his mind. It's hurtful to her that he can see no difference between her and twelve million other people her age. Erica wonders, is Tom smitten with *her* or with *her being twenty-nine?*

It could be that you're typecast as being blonde or being tall or being a doctor or being black. Whatever the single trait in question, you are seen more as a possessor of that trait than as a person.

3. *Conditionality*

Any sense that you get from another person that "you'd

better not change," that he likes you only on condition that you stay as you are, suggests a Projection.

Just out of college, Melissa was hired by a magazine to assemble the "Going Out Guide" each week. Wendy, the managing editor, liked Melissa very much, and Melissa had genuine feelings for Wendy. Wendy was tops at her job and she taught Melissa generously. Under Wendy's tutelage, Melissa began writing more important columns. Eventually, Melissa was noticed by a competing magazine and offered a job as a lead columnist for a lot more money. Wendy made no counteroffer but wished Melissa the best with apparent affection.

Melissa's been at her new job for three months, and tonight she's going to a formal dinner at the Waldorf Astoria in New York City for an elite group of magazine writers. Wendy will be there.

Melissa has been looking forward to seeing Wendy, and her friends have been saying, "Won't she be proud of you!" But beneath her excitement, Melissa has a gnawing feeling that Wendy won't. She has a sense that Wendy won't be able to accept her as an equal: that she'll see her as an entirely new person, one with whom she may even feel competitive. She liked Melissa as she was, but not as she is.

If Melissa's right, Wendy's Projection on her remains that of "dependent novice," and she's unwilling to appreciate her in any other way.

The conditionality in the way people see us is something we can all become aware of if we let ourselves. The most usual culprits, of course, are our own parents. They may see us as incompetent, needy, unschooled, naive, and it may be hard for them to ever rise above that picture.

Of all the symptoms of a Projection, conditionality is one of the most painful, with its threat of sudden loss to us when we've done nothing to deserve it. In fact, the other person may have always said that he wanted us to be a successful adult, confident and independent—exactly what we have now become and what he is now holding against us.

4. *Artificiality*

This is a real "gut" reaction, and it's not one to be dismissed.

Betty has just met her twenty-eight-year-old son's new girlfriend, Janet. Their conversation was pleasant; Janet was polite and even volunteered information about her family and her educational background that Betty never would have asked for. Janet told Betty how much she loved her son, another bit of information Betty didn't require. Then she asked about Betty's job and listened patiently. She seemed sympathetic when Betty spoke about struggles in business, and she complimented Betty on her successes. Now Betty's home alone, mulling over the experience. She doesn't like Janet, but her own reaction seems unreasonable to her. Would she be jealous of any woman her son got serious about? No, to say that wouldn't be fair to herself.

Going over the evening, Betty recalls Janet's stiff smile and formal manner. It's more apparent now than it was when Betty was trying to connect with the younger woman: Janet was *cultivating* her.

There were topics not to be discussed, that Janet didn't *expect* from her: Betty felt censored. Janet winced when Betty mentioned that she'd been going out with a man for two years.

It's getting clearer. The evening was artificial because Janet made no effort to meet the real *person*. She was speaking to her Projection of Betty as "Michael's mother," some matron of the middle class whom she had to meet and captivate.

The sense of artificiality during an experience with someone is an excellent clue that a Projection is at work, but a clue that we are often ready to discount. There's an impulse to say of an experience that felt artificial, "It must have been *my* fault." Many women in Betty's place would have blamed themselves for the faulty connection, cursed themselves for being out of touch with the younger generation, and resolved to try harder next time.

5. *Feeling underestimated*

Mary and Arthur are connecting well and decide to live together, but as soon as they do, things begin to change. Mary was more than acceptable to Arthur as someone he dated and slept with, but now that they've rented an apartment together, it's another story. He tells her not to use the VCR until he explains it to her and then asks her to demonstrate that she really understands how it works; he suggests that she take her elderly dog to obedience school, because "no one who knows about dogs lets them sleep on the furniture."

In Mary's mind, Arthur is idiosyncratic, and this is a period of readjustment and compromise. She finds many of his complaints irritating but decides that it's not worth arguing about trivialities, so she defers in most cases and hopes that he'll settle in. A crisis comes, however, after Arthur accuses her of breaking the new telephone-answering machine. Mary has a dream that Arthur is berating her in public, in the center of a shopping mall, telling the passersby how inept she is.

She wakes up knowing that things have gone too far. Mary was assuming that the problem was altogether Arthur's: that he was overfastidious and picky. He is these things, but the real problem is his Projection of Mary as "heavy handed and incapable." Her recognition that she has been systematically underestimated leads her to spot the Projection.

You can usually tell when another person is regularly underestimating you, because you constantly feel like saying things like, "Why do you think you have to explain that to me?" "Why don't you trust me?" "Why did you ask Joan for her suggestion when I just gave you the solution?" "How many times are you going to ask me if I understand this?"

Most people will find this one of the easier signals to recognize.

6. *Hurtful Humor*

Myra, an unmarried woman in her twenties, worked as a manicurist in a men's hair salon. When she started the job, she made an effort to get along with the male stylists and managers and went along with their "kidding":

"That's a nice dress. Didn't you wear it yesterday? Hope you had a good evening."

"Gee, Myra, why isn't a pretty girl like you married? Having too good a time?"

She hoped that such jokes would pass and she'd be accepted as "one of the boys," but the humor didn't stop; instead, it escalated and became blatantly insulting. One day, when Myra was on the verge of tears, it struck her that Alice, the other woman manicurist, was subjected to no such kidding. Alice was "difficult," and the men knew it.

Myra discussed it all with Alice, who said that the men had tried their "humor" on her too, but she had stopped them in their tracks and threatened to quit if they continued.

"I'd rather be thought of as an oversensitive woman than as a slut," Alice said.

Myra was shocked when she realized that far from coming to see her as a "regular guy," the men were viewing her tolerance as an admission of promiscuity and an *invitation* for them to continue the innuendoes. She had unwittingly nurtured their Projection of her as a slut.

If you are repeatedly hurt by someone's brand of

"humor," something is amiss. That person has a wrong impression of you, and they will keep pushing you, strengthening their Projection and reducing you in their own eyes as long as you let them.

7. Surprise

A woman tells her older brother that she's been accepted at medical school and he's astonished. A man cries in front of his wife after he learns that his best friend has had a near-fatal heart attack, and his wife is astounded and a little disgusted at his reaction. A woman of twenty is shocked when her divorced mother announces that she's going on vacation with a man.

In each case, *the surprise betrays a Projection.* What's so amazing about a young woman going to medical school? Plenty, if you don't think she's very bright or your Projection of women in general is that they can't go very far mentally. And why should a wife be surprised at her husband's feeling so deeply about a friend he loves? To some degree, she doesn't know her own husband: she has projected on him only raw, unemotional strength and has never let herself see the depth of his emotional life, his tenderness. And the girl's Projection of her mother—doubtless it was that of a sexless, selfless adult, perhaps one who lives only for her children.

From people's surprise, we may learn how they really view us. Their surprise indicates that they see us in one way, unwaveringly, and that something they are now hearing or seeing suggests a radical departure—that we are not living up to their Projection.

Note that surprise is a reaction *at an early stage.* When a Projection has evolved to its ultimate form, it may be that nothing we do can surprise the person who holds the Projection. By that time, the person has trained himself to assimilate anything he hears as a fact consistent with what he already believes, or even as evidence supportive of it.

A man holds the Projection that his daughter, Jill, is "flighty and not very intelligent." When she announces her engagement to a capable and accomplished young man, her father tells his wife in private, "I guess he's interested in her for sex."

When Jill, who is an art historian, has a publisher accept her manuscript as a lead book, her father assumes that Jill paid someone else to write it for her. After repeated successes by his daughter, her father concludes, "Boy, they've really lowered standards, haven't they! I guess this generation just isn't very discerning."

In short, contradictory evidence becomes less and less admissible as a Projection matures, and therefore surprises become increasingly rare.

8. *What a person says*

Things people say give us information about the sorts of Projections they tend to form, and possibly about Projections they're already forming about us. The inferences we make from another's own words are helpful in corroborating the meaning of some of the other signals.

How someone talks about others or about himself can tell us a lot.

A man describes a neighbor of his as unstable because he's been divorced. *You* are divorced and he knows it. He's never criticized you directly, but such remarks should put you on guard as to how he may see you. Apparently, he sees all divorced people as "unbalanced."

A woman who has just turned forty comments on how old and unattractive she's getting. "Being forty is not the same as being young." Her forty-two-year-old best friend, a widow eager to rebuild her life, is demoralized by this comment until she thinks it over. Her friend may project "elderliness" on their age group, but that has nothing to do with *her* or with the reality. Because she recognizes the assertion as only a Projection, she can go full speed ahead with her sailing lessons, with her scheduled cruise, and with her new relationship.

Another way we can spot a Projection from what people say is to take into account their own life story. What's past is prologue.

Arnold's girlfriend describes her ex-husband and two previous lovers as "enormously disappointing." She tells him a little about her past; she is still smarting from the immaturity of her former husband, who seemed incapable of loving anyone. And, according to her, so was the fellow she was with at the party where Arnold met her—too many faults, too attached to his mother, and not nearly the man she thought he would be.

But Arnold feels good about winning the competition. He kisses her goodnight and is happy she seems to like him; she's quite attractive, and he feels proud of his perform-ance. He feels masculine.

Instead of feeling proud to be an exception, Arnold should be wary of being the next victim of his girlfriend's relentless disappointment. It would appear that during a relationship with a man, she comes to see him as failing her. Why? Well, maybe she picks the wrong men, but her record suggests that she may be seeing people through a faulty lens. It could be that she sees men as "built-in protectors," and that any lapse on their part makes her feel neglected. It would be wise for Arnold to take stock of his whole experience with her, checking for other signals that, in-deed, a Projection is operating.

Also, people verbalize expectations of others that are so strong as to suggest a Projection:

"Well, I don't think a woman should ever weigh over a hundred and fifteen pounds, no matter what her age or height."

"I don't see why a teenager has to drive a car."

"Only hire people who've been in their last job at least three years; if they want to move before that, there's something wrong with them."

If someone in your life expresses opinions in this peremptory way, he's very likely projecting a high demand for conformity. He expects people to play their assigned roles, whatever he perceives them to be, without deviation. Dogmatic statements about what people should do are a strong sign of Projection.

9. *What other people say*

Sometimes, what close friends of the person say can give you evidence that corroborates your hunches as to his Projection.

Jackie is at her boyfriend's house, and two of his friends drop over for brunch. They don't pay much attention to her, and one of them brings up the subject of Jackie's boyfriend's last amour. "She was really capable. She's going places in that business." At the end of the afternoon, both guests forget to say good-bye to Jackie. Maybe they don't think they'll be seeing her again and it doesn't matter. If Jackie's boyfriend has also been treating her cavalierly, then their blithe treatment of her may imply that he's given them the idea that he sees her as "only a fill-in."

Men, jockeying for top positions in industry, have long known a truth that women would do well to learn, too. In the "old boys'" club, it's common for a man to act friendly toward someone he's stabbing in the back. Your rival's comradeship at the country club may be an attempt to disarm you. But, if you watch *his wife's treatment of you,* it may reveal what he's hiding from you but has confided to her. She's less schooled at concealment than he is.

It's like observing the face of someone who's watching another player's cards at a poker game. That onlooker's expression may tell you what the player himself has taken pains to mask from you.

But be careful in what you conclude from such evidence alone. The third party may have his own motives for his treatment of you. (The guests at brunch may be jealous that their friend lucked out in falling in love; the wife of your business associate may be bitter because she's disappointed and feels you're outclassing her husband.) Use this signal *only* in conjunction with others.

10. *Being misinterpreted*

The last three signals that we want to mention are apt to be dead certain indicators of a Projection, but the kind that is very evolved and that will be hard to budge. You may receive these messages faintly early on, but they're as vivid as skywriting later in the game.

Being misinterpreted, not once but regularly, can indicate that a person has his own theory about who you are. Whatever you do seems to support his theory. He latches on to some trait of yours, which you may or may not have, and attributes everything you do to that trait, misinterpreting everything in its service.

For instance, Linda's boss, Dick, views her as "wildly ambitious, deadly, and out to get his job." Dick is slightly younger than Linda, the job means everything to him—he goes to the office on weekends and spends whole nights preparing for meetings. Linda does much more with far less effort, and her good spirit builds the morale of her co-workers and makes the clients ask for her.

Linda's boss has been placed above her because he's a man and she's a woman. But of course, that's not *Dick's* fault; the prejudice comes from higher up in the company. Linda has made up her mind to work with Dick cooperatively until she finds a job elsewhere, which shouldn't be difficult.

Meanwhile, everything Linda does is misconstrued by Dick. When she makes a good speech to the sales force, she's trying to charm them. When she stays late to help Dick finish a project, she's doing it to appear self-sacrificing to the company president. When she spends her own money on birthday presents for her staff, it's because she's bribing them to lie against Dick. Dick is incapable of seeing that such acts spring from Linda's goodwill and desire to make the best of an imperfect situation.

This sort of misinterpretation is a serious sign of a deeply ensconced Projection.

Every Projection includes some degree of misinterpretation—of who we are, of what is special about us. But to use misinterpretation as an indicator, you must look for misconstruing of your motives. You get a sense that black is white and white is black, and the more you try to clarify your position, the more misunderstood you are.

11. *Straining*

The discovery that you yourself are struggling, that you've been acting unnaturally or trying to prove yourself, can tell you that you're up against a strong Projection.

It's a curious truth that our responses often precede our recognition. We are capable of automatically trying to neutralize a danger before we've even identified it. We feel some distress, some agitation. If we look at our own behavior, we can isolate those actions we've been taking against the danger and backtrack to discover the danger itself.

"Why have I felt compelled to name-drop? I don't usually do that. I'm feeling like a nothing. This man must be *making* me feel that way by telling me I've never seen a country house like his, and I'd better buy some new clothes to meet all his friends. He sees me as 'an unsophisticated, socially impaired nonentity.' "

"Why do *I* always pay for dinner when I go out with my

friend Jack? He never offers to split the check. And I lent him my lawnmower even though I *knew* he takes forever to return things and I'd need it next weekend. Damn it, I'm turning myself inside out for that guy, and he doesn't seem to think there's anything unusual about it. I think he'd be mad if I *didn't* go out of my way for him. It's as if I owe him half of everything I've got. Just because I have a business that is finally paying off and he got fired from his last two jobs, he sees me as lucky and as his natural benefactor.''

The sequence is straightforward. You recognize that you're overreacting or trying to accomplish something in a conversation or in a situation that you shouldn't have to. Your analysis leads you to see that the other person has been putting pressure of some kind on you—forcing you to defend yourself or prove something about yourself. You've been playing into his hands by trying to disabuse him of his Projection: the woman in the first example name-dropped to show that she was not the inexperienced homebody her date imagined her to be.

With Jack, the freeloader, his friend has been alternately giving in to him and making excuses to fend him off. Realizing how uncomfortable he's felt with Jack, he now sees that Jack has been treating him as part of his economy.

The sense that you are straining can serve as a clue to what the other person is doing to you, and what he is projecting.

The great thing about making this identification is that even if you can't correct him, your discovery instantly enables you to stop trying to prove yourself. The strain is gone.

12. *Feeling of hopelessness*

Hopelessness is a feeling you will have to some degree with all Projections. But it becomes profound when a Projection is ironclad.

Kate's best friend, Anna, is desperately unhappy with her husband. Every day she has some new atrocity to report. He's cut her out of their joint bank account, he's insisting their daughter go to a college that's not her choice, he's rude to Anna's friends, and he won't let her go on business trips necessary for her work. True, Anna's life *is* miserable, but it is *Kate* who feels utterly hopeless after they talk.

Looking more closely, Kate realizes that even when she has sympathized with Anna, Anna has rebutted everything she's said and has put her down. Worse yet, Anna has even implied that she is ruthless and not the sort of person Anna herself would ever want to be.

She's asked Kate, "What should I do?" and Kate has volunteered suggestions. "You can't let your husband dominate your daughter. You've got to stand up for her."

But Anna has come back at her, "Look, he's her father, and I don't want to argue with my husband the way *you* argue with yours. I've heard you two."

On another occasion, Kate told her, "You've got to go on your business trips or you'll never get promoted."

Anna has replied by saying that she couldn't be that cruel to her husband, and run out on him like that. *"You* could do that, I know. But I can't."

Examining her despair, Kate comes to appreciate that Anna's Projection of her is that of a "cold, calculating person who would stop at nothing." By contrast, Anna apparently sees herself as a "delicate angel, suffering as a good person should in order to make things work."

Anna's was a deep and matured Projection. No matter what Kate did, Anna saw her as the villain of the piece. Even though Kate has given Anna her time and her best effort, Kate looks no better to her than if she had refused Anna's phone calls. No wonder Kate feels hopeless.

In the early stages of a Projection, your feelings of hopelessness may come only in moments. You run the risk of suppressing them. "Maybe I'm just depressed." But those glimpses of hopelessness might tell you a lot about how you're being viewed by the other person, if you investigated them.

PROJECTIONS WITH
AN ELEMENT OF TRUTH

It's especially hard to spot a Projection when the person sees something in you that is *really there.*

Vivien is very involved with a number of friends and projects. She's a passionate person, maybe a little high-strung, and she tends to come home at night all wound up. Many people depend on her—as someone who understands their problems, as the person who can find the right expert for any emergency, as an organizer who can list for them what they need to do and suggest priorities. All of this is in addition to Vivien's considerable job responsibilities, and many evenings she voices her latest concerns almost before she's inside the door. Relaxing at home has never been her specialty.

Understandably, her husband, Eric, gets jarred by her intensity. He'd be happier if she made herself less available to others and centered more on him. Though she loves him and is loyal to him, she has not given him nearly enough unbroken time.

Recently, Eric accused her of driving him crazy, almost as though she were doing it intentionally. He implied that she deliberately diversified herself because she's never been committed to the marriage. He even accused her of planning to leave him. Last night, he shouted at her that she doesn't know what it is to love a man. His Projection of her is that she "takes men lightly and abandons them."

Vivien went into shock over what he said and over how he apparently sees her. Now she asks herself, "Which one of us is crazy?" Forcing herself to make an honest evaluation, she has to admit that she has been keeping him at arm's length by interposing so many other concerns. He has plenty of right to complain and to feel neglected. In fact, she's even glad he *does* feel so strongly. She feels terrible. There's certainly a lot of truth in what he says.

And yet there's a lot of falsehood, too. It's not that she *wanted* to push him away. Moreover, he has no idea how much she does love him and how willing she is to change. He seems to assume that she's always been this way and would never wish to be any different. If Eric had any hope for her, he could have told her how upset he was when he first felt abandoned due to her behavior. His Projection is the *attribution* of coldness and deliberateness to what she's done. Although his observations are accurate, the Projection itself, like *all* Projections, is an untruth. It is a perception of Vivien's motives that Eric has himself imported.

The hardest Projections to deal with are those that fuse with reality. There are elements of truth in what the person sees. But he's blown up these "truths" or isolated them from the rest of your character. There is a lot to you that he is not seeing.

AXIOM XI: A Projection that is fused with reality contains two elements: The person attributes to you motivations that are *not* truly yours. And the person feels a hopelessness about your ability or desire to change, which is *not* warranted.

HISTORICAL
OVERLAYS
___

Ascribing motives to others that they do not have and feeling hopeless about another's ability or willingness to change, both have roots in the early history of the person projecting.

Eric had parents who *truly* neglected him. They favored his older brother, an athlete and an excellent student. When as a little boy Eric broke his only pair of glasses, they were slow to replace them. He grew up assuming that people didn't love him or treasure him. He was ready to see Vivien as one more person who didn't give a damn, and to pounce on evidence that seemed to suggest that.

He had learned early in his history that any attempts to get people to cherish him were futile so it wasn't even worth the effort. Moreover, since he was utterly dependent on his parents for love, attention, food, shelter, and education, and had no conceivable alternative, the idea that they *didn't* cherish him was disastrous.

To Eric, the implications of being unwanted—neglected—were overwhelming. As a child, he could not choose another family, but was at the mercy of adults he could not get through to. In adulthood, he still responded to any kind of neglect from someone close to him with a hopeless, catastrophic feeling. Vivien's slighting him—as by answering the phone during dinner—would unnerve him more than it should. The idea of Vivien's wanting to change because she deeply loved him was simply not in his psychic lexicon. Recognizing neglect was tantamount to receiving a death sentence.

Certainly, some of the neglect that Eric identified was

real, but much that the neglect implied in his mind was false.

There are people who project good intentions onto their harshest critics because their parents' only way of showing involvement was to criticize their failings. Based on that Projection they choose friends, maybe even a lover, who carp and nag, disdaining those who see what's best in them.

A woman married to a gentle man with an occasional flash of temper may project on him the physical violence that her father showed when she was a child. A man may project elegance and social skills on a woman who is morbidly concerned with "what people think," just as his mother was.

All Projections have historical antecedents. But in a Projection that is fused with reality, these antecedents afford your best way of spotting the Projection.

AXIOM XII: Look to a person's history if he seems to be obsessed with some aspect of you to the exclusion of the rest. It's likely to be a trait perceived in a parent during childhood, one they felt they had to live with, that troubled them, or that was central in their lives.

WHEN THE EVIDENCE
POINTS TO A PROJECTION
——

When you've accumulated evidence that someone is projecting on you, your first impulse may be to stand by and do nothing, to let things pass, to bide your time. You may hope that the person will correct his mistaken view of you by himself. Before long, the truth *must* become obvious to him. How can anyone go on ignoring the facts?

"My mother can't possibly go on seeing me as a little kid after my baby is born."

"I've been running the department for three months since my supervisor got sick and everything's going smoothly. The boss will *have* to see I'm ready for the management training program; that I'm no longer just a clerk."

Another early impulse is to make excuses. "Perhaps what my business partner did today is just an exception. Tomorrow he'll see that I'm not just 'the drudge.' "

"My lover only *seems* indifferent to me; he's overfocused on himself now because he's up for that big job. He'll take an interest in me after it's resolved. The problem will blow over, and I'll be glad if I haven't made a fuss, and accused him of just seeing me as 'the maid.' "

You may think you're excusing the other person, but part of what you're doing is exempting yourself from having to face a confrontation and the temporary discomfort of dealing with a Projection. There's a thin line between tolerance and cowardice.

No matter how you look at it, simply being who you are won't suffice. You'll have to ferret out the Projection and take action to stop it.

SUMMARY

The twelve signals for spotting a Projection are all accompanied by some degree of personal discomfort. Just as physical pain warns us that something is amiss in the body, these feelings of emotional "not-rightness"—the sense of being somehow "off-balance" when with a certain person—may serve to tell you that the person is systematically not seeing who you really are.

It is crucial to be attuned to these signals, and to resist any impulse to dismiss them. You must be particularly vigilant when dealing with Projections that contain some element of truth. Remember, the earlier you spot a Projection, the more you can do to dispel it.

When you're sure that a Projection is operating, you can also be sure that the other person is *treating* you in accordance with his Projection and that each act of his is further strengthening the Projection, further persuading him that he is right about you.

It's obvious that a person who sees you wrongly will treat you wrongly. But only through an understanding of the Projection Principle can you see a more subtle truth: When you get the person to treat you better, he will, as a result, see you as you want him to.

In the next chapter, we will present the master plan you must set in motion the instant you spot another person's Projection.

4

HOW CAN YOU HALT A PROJECTION?

This chapter concerns strategy. How do you break in once you realize that a person is beginning to see you in a detrimental way?

If you're one of the great majority who find open confrontations distasteful, what's ahead won't be easy. In opposing the Projection, you'll very possibly make the other person anxious or angry, and you'll suffer accordingly.

It helps to remember, however, that you're going to suffer less in opposing the Projection now than you would if you let things go on as they are. If you live with a Projection, you are living a lie. At best, you'll have a distant relationship, you'll feel continuously misunderstood, and you'll see yourself as something of a fraud. At worst, you'll feel you're a stranger to the other person, or if you try to change to conform with his Projection, a stranger to yourself. The apprehensiveness that haunts you amounts to a running fear that the person will discover that you are not who he thinks you are, and will dismiss you from his life.

If you love someone, or if, as with a difficult boss or relative, you need the person in your life, your confronting him is bound to be unsettling. But you are investing in your future. You'll nearly always be effective, and the relationship will improve. In the rare cases where the other person refuses to give you better treatment and won't see you differently, at least *you'll* know who you're dealing with. You won't have lost anything, since a relationship with anyone who simply refuses to acknowledge who you are is hopeless. And knowing you've done all you can provides relief—you can stop banging your head against the wall.

Keep all this in mind, especially if you have to get tough. And remember that you have no alternative but to step in.

USE THE LEAST FORCE POSSIBLE

When you intervene, you should act with just enough force to get the other person to treat you differently—no more, no less. You simply want him to change that part of his behavior which is poisoning his mind against you. Unless he's been insulting you outright, he may have no idea that he's been doing anything amiss. His joking or defaults or the way he refers to you may seem innocent to him, and very possibly you'll find him more than receptive to what you ask. If he is to attribute better qualities to you, he must change his behavior, but why provoke anger or fear in him if he had no bad intentions?

Only if the person refuses to treat you differently, or repeatedly "forgets," will you need to be more blunt. You may not have to do very much more than point out the problem. However, if the person simply won't stop, even after you've told him how important it is to you, you may have to get tough.

In the extreme case, you may even have to threaten to end the relationship. And it is important that you not be bluffing. It may be a lot better to quit the job or end the friendship, sometimes even to terminate a marriage, than to allow yourself to be whittled away over time.

But remember, don't keep pushing beyond *any* point where you get a response. You're not out to elicit a signed confession. At this stage, you're not even asking the person to *see* the implications of his behavior; all you're asking him to do is to treat you in a way that allows the best possible outcome for both of you. As the Projection Principle promises, once you get the right treatment, the rest will fall into place.

AXIOM XIII: When you intervene to stop a Projection, use just enough force to deter the harmful behavior, no more, no less. As soon as the person agrees to what you're asking, *relax the pressure.*

At best, we patrol our image the way an ideal police force would protect a city. Our interventions are only occasional, and nearly all of those are quiet and unobtrusive. By showing calm determination early, we may save ourselves the need to be vehement later.

We're about to detail a seven-step sequence for halting a Projection. Most of the time, you won't have to go past the third or fourth step. On occasion, if you've let a Projection go too far before trying to head it off, you may have to go to the fifth or sixth step. In the worst case scenario, you may have to go to the bitter end.

BREAKING IN: THE STRATEGY

————

1. *Pinpointing the harmful behavior*

You are now aware that someone is Projecting on you. You discovered this fact through noticing one or more of the twelve signals mentioned in the last chapter. You should now look at the warning signals, *the very ones that led you to see the Projection in the first place,* and ask yourself the question "What is the person doing that makes me feel this way?"

For instance, "Why do I feel that John is underestimating me? He certainly doesn't see me as a potential vice-president of sales."

Answers will come to mind at once: "He doesn't ask me for advice the way he used to." "He makes unilateral decisions and tells me about them later." These are among the behaviors he must change if he is revise his present Projection of you as "unpromotable." As you continue to watch the interaction, you'll find other instances of John's pejorative behavior—bypassing you, *underestimating* you. Be sure to look for things he *doesn't* do, but ought to, as well as for things he does toward you.

Your own uncomfortable feelings—the alarm signals already mentioned—should alert you to look for the treatment that is inducing those bad feelings.

In another example, a woman has a vague disquietude—the "not me" feeling—but has trouble tracing it. It's the end of the evening, and Julia has given an elaborate dinner party for her boyfriend and two couples close to him whom she has just met for the first time. Everyone had fun, and the guests were lavish in their praise of Julia's cooking and her apartment. This delighted her because she is a skilled cook and she has just redecorated her apartment herself. But now that she's alone with her boyfriend, she feels inexplicably despondent. Something feels terribly wrong. The thought flashes into her mind, "He doesn't know who I am."

He has done nothing overtly wrong during the evening, though she was somewhat hurt that he didn't join in the praise of her cooking. "In fact," Julia thinks, "he didn't even seem to understand why they were bringing it up. And he looked bored when they talked about my apartment."

Then it hits her.

Thinking back over the day, she realizes that a comment he made early in the afternoon, while she was cooking, bothered her. "I can't wait for my friends to meet you and find out you're a neurologist. I haven't told them yet." He had made several such comments during the week. The behavior provoking Julia's discomfort was her boyfriend's esteeming her for her medical expertise and the status it implied, to the exclusion of the rest of her, which was rich and varied and which she hoped was lovable. She now knows what to look out for and resolves to identify any such behavior in the future—to end his Projection of her as "prestigious neurologist" rather than as "woman."

Often your reactions to projective treatment will set in slowly, especially if you're given to pretending that unpleasant things aren't happening when they are. If the treatment appears on the surface to be complimentary, it may be especially hard to construe as the real threat it is.

Once you've caught onto a Projection and spotted some of the actions supporting it, it becomes easier to find others.

The more you know about the nature of the Projection, the more you know where to look.

2. *Spotlighting the behavior*

The second step is to show the person what he's doing, to make him aware of the behavior that you don't like. Think of speaking to him at this stage lightly but clearly, as if you were simply putting a spotlight on the destructive action.

Letting him know may be easy; the hard part right now is to limit yourself to doing this and nothing more. You may feel a temptation to unload the whole of your grievance on him, to tell him how much you've suffered, and how unfair he has been. But at this point, you've got to give him a chance. Dignity and even practicality require that you approach him cleanly, even if he hasn't been fair with you. Unless you remain calm, *you'll* feel like a hysteric and the one at fault.

For instance, Gary is the photo editor for a home furnishings magazine. His boss has started asking him to take notes for him at meetings, even when he's at the table himself. This makes Gary look like the boss's secretary to the rest of the editorial staff, and it hampers him from actively participating in the meeting and from doing his best thinking. Somehow, the boss has relegated Gary to an inferior role and takes for granted that he won't mind. Ever since he hired that pushy new design person, it's been getting worse. The boss has been turning to her for the answers that Gary used to give. Perhaps Gary's already let it go on for too long, which is why it is so hurtful—and why he feels so furious.

Gary would like to tell the boss that he deserves a lot better for his three years of dedication. He may have fantasies of reminding his boss of how he came through when he needed him, staying late night after night and even postponing a vacation. But it's important that he not whine or complain. Since this is Gary's first time confronting the boss, he owes him simplicity and an opportunity to change his Projection of Gary as "flunky."

Spotlighting the behavior consists simply of making the other person aware of it. Gary might say to his boss, "Harvey, this is no fun. These days all I'm doing is acting as scribe. It's hard for me to concentrate on the look of the next issue, or to come up with any really creative shots when I'm so tuned out of the editorial meetings. Maybe you could have one of the interns take the notes."

In another instance, we have seen a relationship saved when a subordinate commented warmly yet firmly on his boss's insensitive behavior: "My! You're certainly in a grumpy mood today." His boss replied, "Oh! am I? Yes, I guess I am. Sorry." And from there he went on to treat the person differently, gradually dropping his Projection of that employee as "a robot, there only to serve him." He was even thankful to have this pointed out. The subordinate helped reverse the ingraining of the Projection by speaking up.

Another employee, either too frightened or too angry to speak up, might have allowed the mistreatment to progress until the boss had convinced himself that the employee deserved only scoffs because he counted so little.

Spotlighting the other person's behavior is usually done best by simply telling him what he's doing.

Against your mate's Projection of you as "supporter and therapist rather than lover," you might say, "Darling, you must have asked me nineteen questions in a row. What about me? Where's my space?"

To combat a Projection of you as "eternal protégé," you might have occasion to say, "I agree I couldn't have done it without you. But your constant reminders of that fact don't make me feel any better about myself."

To a lover who doesn't see you as you are, you might say, "Sweetheart, sometimes you talk to me as if I'm an employee."

And to a mate whose Projection is that you're "socially awkward," you might say, "I'll do my best to get along with your folks, I promise. You don't have to keep mentioning it every ten minutes."

Recently a friend of mine, a college history teacher, spotlighted with obvious humor the behavior of a colleague who had told him eleven times not to say anything to anyone about a new job the colleague had been offered. The colleague was projecting "a loose tongue" on my friend.

Finally my friend replied, "I'll isolate myself until it's all official. I won't even go home to my wife tonight in case I talk in my sleep."

The other fellow saw his point and replied at once, "I'm sorry, Marty. I know you won't say anything. You never break a confidence. I guess I'm just on pins and needles."

After that, the incident was forgotten.

3. *Asking the person to stop*

If merely mentioning the behavior doesn't help, *ask* the person to stop, with or without giving him a reason:

"Darling, please don't ask me any more questions for a while."

"Please stop reminding me of the different ways you helped me. It undermines my feeling that I can do things on my own."

It's important once again that your request carry no extra baggage. Sarcasm in particular disposes the person to resist doing what you want.

Avoid implications that the other person *wants* to do you

injury: "You're addressing me like an employee because you're trying to turn me into your private secretary. *I know you think that's the only thing women are good for.*"

Also, refrain from including descriptions of how much the person's behavior makes you suffer: "I was up all night thinking about how badly you treat me. You're always afraid I'm going to blunder around your parents and it makes me miserable." Even if this is so, portraying yourself as so vulnerable won't help you gain status with another person.

Speaking up without rancor or self-pity may not be easy, but such attitudes never enhance relationships. Rancor drives people away, and those in whom you induce pity will hold you in contempt.

4. *Making clear the alternative treatment you want*

You may have to spell out what you want the person to do. Sometimes you may be asking for better treatment point blank:

"Darling, instead of constantly asking me questions about what you should do, can't we just enjoy each other for a while, the way we used to?"

"Please treat me like an equal. I'm on your level now. We both run companies."

"Since neither of us is working for the other, please stop the orders and let's just share the chores."

"Why don't you just trust me when we go visiting? I'm sure I'll do fine without your instructions."

In other cases, you may want *different* treatment, which the other person may not consider better.

For instance, Jenny's husband is far too deferential. He projects on her a "stormy disposition and an unfair, accusatory nature," which isn't hers at all. He says to her things like, "Please don't be angry with me, but I don't see things the way you do."

And at another time, "Now don't get mad, but I decided to do it a little differently when I was there."

It's as if he expected her to beat him or to feel utter contempt toward him for differing with her. Almost surely, whether he knows it or not, he's building a case in his own mind that she's impossible to deal with. Unless he stops treating her this way, he'll soon create an intense fear of displeasing her—very likely akin to the fear he had of displeasing a parent. Eventually, through no fault of Jenny's, he'll find it a strain to be with her: he will be the loser and so will she.

When Jenny asks him to change his behavior, she might include some explanation: "Please don't assume that I'm always going to be angry when we disagree about something. It's not fair. I'm not so unreasonable; you don't have to talk to me that way."

Still subtler are cases in which you must ask the person to stop doing something which he thought was for your benefit. To him, it may even look as if you're asking for *worse* treatment.

Fred, concerned about getting older, sees his young wife, Sybil, as a "goddess who is easily displeased." He buys gifts for her that he can't afford, he dumps his own friends and sees only hers, he shortens business trips so that he can help her in small ways. She truly loves him and senses the robustness going out of their relationship. She feels a distance between them; one that *he* is creating.

It behooves Sybil to tell him she doesn't want such sacrifices: "Please, Fred, there's no need to spend that kind of money." Or, "Fred, stay in California the extra day and go to the meeting. I can take the dog to be groomed without you. Let's divide the chores equally."

Only by confronting him and asking him not to sacrifice unduly can she stop him from feeling that if he fails to do things for her, she'll leave him. When we allow a person to curtail himself too much for our sake, the eventual result is a worse life for him and the harmful Projection onto us that we exist to sap his resources. This Projection onto us can destroy love and friendship and in the end induce the other person to resent us, perhaps even to retaliate.

Especially with a person who is well-intentioned, as in this last case, we might explain our reason for the request, using the Projection Principle. "I know you do so much because you care about me. But I don't like seeing you make so many sacrifices. They're not necessary. Besides, you're giving yourself a wrong impression of what I really want in life. I'd rather see you happy than denying yourself things for me."

Or suppose a friend begins sparing you painful facts—for your own good. Maybe he considers you "easily panicked." He's had a serious illness and imagines that if he tells you the details and the risks facing him, you'll become overly distraught.

You may explain that only if he confides in you and teaches himself that you are indeed his ally will the relationship prosper. By asking him to *trust* you, you are cutting off a harmful Projection of you as "susceptible to the vapors."

5. *Getting past the resistances*

No matter how diplomatic we are, people don't always respond well when they are asked to change. Some will bristle at anything that sounds like a criticism. Even when what you're asking for seems trivial, it may be hard for the other person to comply with it. Often with even a simple request, you will encounter deep and irrational opposition, and you've got to be prepared for it.

Familiarity with some of the usual forms of resistance can help you anticipate them and deal with them. There are five forms of resistance that we want to talk about: *reality, humor, oversensitivity, ignorance* and *emotional collapse.*

First, let's look at *reality*—the argument that no remark can be mistreatment if it's truthful. For instance, a friend of yours constantly comments in front of other people that you love to sleep, that you're slow getting ready for appointments, and that you're usually late. Her Projection on you is that you're "lazy and careless." She also believes that she can push you around in public. You ask the "friend" not to say those things, especially when you're with other people. To your astonishment, the friend replies, "Why not? They're true."

Don't try to rebut the charges; their veracity isn't the point. Be blunt: "I'm asking you not to say these things if you *are* my friend. They're hurtful, and there's nothing good in them."

You can do nothing more than this. Don't counterpunch: "You're fat and your last three lovers left you because you don't have orgasms." Never justify another person's unfair tactic by using it yourself.

Anyone who goes around firing off negatives simply because they're true is clearly on a spree of anger.

Another resistance device you'll encounter is *humor*— often signalled by the claim, "I was only kidding."

"Why are you so touchy about being called scatterbrained? I was just fooling around."

"Can't you take a joke? You *know* you're not messy."

"You *know* you're not a slut, so why get upset?"

"Didn't people ever kid around with you? Haven't you got any sense of humor at all? Did you think I was *really* calling you stupid?"

The joker would prey on any doubts you harbor about having a sense of humor and about its correlates: "Maybe I'm not worldly enough, I don't know how people act in the big time; I'm not loose, I'm too serious." The joker wants you to think that you're making a mountain out of a molehill and that if you think it over, you'll see that no harm was intended. This is what makes humor so effective as a masking device: naturally you're tense whenever you feel things are going wrong, so there's some validity in the charge that you're rigid and losing your sense of humor. And, even at best, it's sometimes hard to know when people are teasing you.

However, you don't have to be sure. Possibly you *did* miss the humor when he called you scatterbrained or said you were a slob. If so, the worst he can say is that you don't enjoy a good joke at your own expense. So what? He can hardly hate you for that unless he hates you already. You've got to be ready to live with the charge that you're humorless. After all, it's only *his* opinion.

Let's say you've just asked the person to stop doing something, and he replies, "I was only kidding. Can't you take a joke?"

You might respond, "Not this one. I wish you'd stop."

Still he pushes you. "Come on. Don't be so serious."

"You may be kidding. But that's not my kind of humor."

Some of these characters really think they are being funny. In other cases, there's no humor even intended. Only when confronted does the person try to cover his tracks by pretending he was kidding. But he obviously wasn't. He has tried to run over you. Now you get tough— for instance, you threaten to go to a higher-up at work if he won't stop joking about your poor English. Then he pretends you missed his joke.

"Don't get so upset. I wasn't serious."

"Of course not. Don't you worry. Forget it. I wasn't serious either."

You know he wasn't kidding, and he knows you weren't and that may be good enough. It may be in your best interests to let him save face by pretending he was.

Of course, humor works both ways. Just as the other

person may package his abuse in a light wrapping, *you* can use it to make your very strong objection tolerable.

For example, at the company sales conference Rhonda is told that there will be a closed session on Sunday for the sales force only. As Art Director, she is asked, along with the rest of the firm, not to show up until seven o'clock in the evening for cocktails and dinner. Rhonda arrives right on time, but the male Sales Manager, who is highly competitive with her, greets her caustically by saying, *"We've* been working since eight-thirty this morning. What have *you* been doing all day?"

Rhonda replies, "I've been designing the plaque for your Purple Heart."

The group laughs, but after that the Sales Manager is slower to make snide remarks.

In another instance, Terry always keeps his friend Sven waiting. One day, after Sven has been waiting at the tennis court for what seems like hours, Terry arrives and asks casually, "Been waiting long?"

Sven answers flatly, "I was a little kid when I got here, and now I've grown up and lost my hair."

Many successful people use humor as a device, closing the door on potential trouble lightly wherever they can. Their philosophy is, "I don't have to humiliate another person to accomplish my purpose!"

The third type of resistance used by people whose behavior you challenge is to call you *oversensitive.* Typical ways of doing this are to say, "You're touchy," "You take things too seriously," "You're overreacting."

Characterizing you this way is an attempt to disarm you by shifting the blame. For instance, you know someone who continually talks about himself but hangs up the phone the instant you start to talk about your own life. You've endured this treatment for a long time, but by putting up with it you've only convinced him that you have no feelings or needs of your own. You've encouraged his Projection of you as "just a sounding board" for him.

Finally, when you ask him to face what he's doing, he wonders angrily why you're suddenly overreacting. He asks, "What's eating you all of a sudden?" as if *you're* the one who's off base.

He is saying in effect, "I don't want to deal with your concerns—or even hear about them." If he can persuade himself, or you, that this is *your* problem, then he has disqualified any objection you might make. If you succumb, he can go on rolling right over you. You've forfeited not only your right to complain about what he's doing now but also your right to object to anything he does in the future.

Let's say that he's only recently developed his Projection, that you *are* somewhat oversensitive—that you bristled too soon in this case. It's hard to know for sure, of course, because if he's started rubbing away at you in other ways as well, you *do* feel raw, and many things bother you more than they should.

But even granting that you may be oversensitive, if he is really well-disposed toward you, he ought to consider your comfort. We all go through life honoring other people's sensibilities where we can, and what you're asking for here won't cost the other person that much.

Don't react to his crying "oversensitive," by relenting in your demand. Don't soften as if to prove that you're a sport and can take whatever he dishes out. Don't quit as if to imply that you're strong and that his treatment of you didn't really bother you that much. You won't win his favor by stoicism. Being sensitive is not a sign of weakness. Don't let him embarrass you out of your position.

Remember that real strength begins with sensitivity. Just as a painter couldn't create unless he were sensitive to clashing colors as well as to pleasing ones, you can't expect to get through life without sensitivity to being slighted or otherwise misunderstood. Not that you need to constantly complain, but you should know what's happening and speak out when you see fit. Being able to feel is a mark of strength.

When someone calls you oversensitive, you might well answer, "That's right. I am. So back off!"

Or at the very least, you might say, "That's *your* opinion. Meanwhile please don't treat me like that again."

By the way, a number of Shakespeare's characters prided themselves on their sensibility, regarding it as a virtue. Viola, the heroine of *Twelfth Night,* warns that she is sensitive to "the least sinister usage." You see the same sentiment in Othello: "Thou hast not half the power to do me harm,/ As I have to be hurt." And when MacDuff suffers grievously at the hands of Macbeth, he is told "Dispute it like a man"; to which he replies, "I shall do so;/ But I must also feel it as a man."

Each of us has arrived at a distinct attitude toward our right to be sensitive to injury—to feel it and to talk about it. Those of us who were loved as young children and whose feelings were considered worth paying attention to in the home are likely to have retained access to them. Curiously, utter neglect in childhood also trains us to hear our feelings. When no one listens to us, the good side is that no one tells us not to feel as we do. Neither the emotionally underprivileged nor the emotionally privileged are easily manipulated by the charge that they are oversensitive.

There is one kind of childhood that often gives rise to alienation from feelings. It produces adults not sure of their feelings or of their *right* to take offense when they are hurt; such people, being disposed to mistrust their own instincts, grow up to be easy victims of many undesirable projections.

The home that produces this kind of person is one in

which the parents expect the child to function, to get ahead, to do what's right, but to keep a low profile. They want the child to be liked but not noticed.

The child learns that surface life is safe: were this child to ask "Mommy, do you love me?" the answer would be a perfunctory "Certainly I do," with an implication of "Don't bother me; don't be so sensitive."

In such a home, the inner life has no currency; to try to probe it is to discover the true neglect that pervades the environment. The child grows up, like an army ant, with a much stronger responsibility to the functioning colony than to his own happiness; all seems fine on the surface, and the child might even say he or she is happy. But there is a vague, spectral sense that nothing is right. To the person from this background, to be sensitive is to press one's luck.

Children from such homes, and there are millions of them, grow up characterologically afraid of being "sensitive." If you are one of these, you must learn that being able to feel and make requests is a birthright, the use of which is vital to you if you are to have any influence over the projections of others onto you.

Two other common forms of resistance you may come up against are *ignorance* and *emotional collapse.*

With the first, the person may act astonished. "I meant nothing by it! I had no idea I was hurting you." This may well be true; you can be sure it's true if, now that he *does* know, he stops. You may have no need to go further, having made your point.

A more primitive form of willful ignorance is the assertion, "I do it with everyone." Obviously, this is no justification for anything. You needn't insist that the treatment shouldn't be used with *anyone.* The simple answer to "I do it with everyone" is "Not with me."

With the second, emotional collapse, the person who seemed utterly indifferent to your feelings, or at least oblivious of them, looks stricken and goes into a state of near collapse when you ask for what seems to you like an minor moderation of his behavior. Parents may do this to a child: "You're giving me a heart attack," or, "You don't love me any more."

Still you've got to hold your course; the fragile bully should have no more claim to your forbearance than the aggressive one.

Some people resort to the entire battery of resistance devices if you confront them. For instance, they may at first claim ignorance of what they're doing; then, when you press them and remind them of details, they ask, "Can't you take a joke?" If you say you didn't like the joke, they may then call your sense of humor into question or call you oversensitive; finally, when it becomes obvious that you won't retreat from your request, they collapse or get furious.

Such rapid shifting from one posture to another, without any pause to examine what they've done, nearly always indicates that they sense their own responsibility and don't feel good about having been found out. How much easier it would be for them simply to reconsider what they've been doing and to stop doing it!

When you do prevail and they change, not only do they stop projecting the unwanted picture of you; more than likely they forget whatever charges they made. If a woman was experiencing "joking" abuse on the job and protested that her employers were belittling her, they would almost surely see her as touchy at first. But soon after they quit the "kidding," their Projection of her as "beneath them" would change, and she would no longer look touchy. Rather, she would appear entitled to the respectful treatment she demanded.

When you encounter a very strong resistance, it always stems from a deep personal need on the other person's part.

For instance, Rosalyn politely asks her mother to stop disparaging her for leaving a secure job to take a riskier one with better promise. Her mother calls her "irresponsible."

"Please stop saying that," Rosalyn pleads.

"Well, you obviously are," her mother replies.

It turns out in this case that the mother herself feels unfulfilled and regrets that she never took chances in life or expressed herself in the business world. Her daughter's success has opened up the floodgates of these misgivings and running her daughter down as "irresponsible and opportunistic" is a defense against having to face her own failure in life.

Thus, though Rosalyn does not know it, what seems like a simple request on her part is really a demand that her mother abandon the rationalization she has used for a lifetime to justify her own lack of performance. So long as the mother can condemn her own daughter, she can go on believing that the only ones who succeed in the world are the opportunistic and disloyal, which in turn explains (or more precisely, seems to explain) her own failure.

The victim of the unfair Projection in such cases rarely appreciates why the behavior is so hard to change: that it is crucial to the other person's own psychic balance. These projections offer the staunchest resistance, and it's against them that you'll often have to take the most extreme measures.

6. *Escalation: creating a crisis*

You've used all but your big guns, and now you need them. The other person has *insisted* on your playing a certain role, overruling your objections. You simply refuse to play the role, in no uncertain terms. Your relationship might not survive such a confrontation, but if playing a false role is necessary to preserve it, it's not worth saving anyhow. You have nothing left to lose.

Creating a crisis is a dramatic way of drawing attention to the difference between how you're perceived and who you really are. It's a method you perhaps hoped to avoid, one to employ only after others have been tried to no avail. The person either hasn't listened or has heard you out but dismissed your complaint as trivial or ill-founded. Either way you can see you're losing status fast. Creating a crisis is your last resort if you ever hope to get your point across.

For instance, Celeste's grown-up son and his wife have come to see her as having no life of her own—as old and existing only to serve them. Of course, they have other feelings about her too, but ever since they became parents themselves, they have evolved this Projection that "Celeste's life lacks real significance."

Typical of how they've downgraded her is the way they've dealt with her as a baby-sitter. At first, they treated her as if she were doing them a favor, giving her plenty of notice and thanking her profusely for helping them out. Gradually, however, they began letting things go and calling her nearer to the last minute, regardless of how far in advance they had made their own plans. Then they stopped thanking her altogether. By each act of indifference, they've increased their sense that Celeste has no life of her own and is at their service. As they convinced themselves of this, they became even more disdainful, imposing on her in other ways.

In vain she protested, saying she had other things to do; why didn't they let her know earlier? But her voice seemed to fall on deaf ears. They even commented smugly that the high point in Celeste's life was to see her grandchildren. Because there was some truth in this, she felt stymied by it. But she feared that even her grandchildren, seeing how she was treated, would come to think of her as a second-class citizen in the family.

It's time to create the crisis—not a major one, but a real

one in the other person's life. Remember that once people mistreat you, their actions persuade them of their Projections and you can't stop what they think; you *must* oppose their behavior.

Quietly, Celeste makes plans for next Friday, when she expects she'll be getting a last-minute call to baby-sit. When the call comes she says, "Sorry, Virginia, I can't; I've got somewhere to go . . . Sure, I'd love to talk to Jim, put him on the phone . . . Jimmie, how are you? I saw that wonderful ad your company had in the newspaper yesterday. Boy, they sure are growing. How did Bonnie do in that nursery school interview? Tell me about it . . . Isn't that wonderful! . . . Tonight? . . . Oh! No, I can't. I'm sorry . . . But I just didn't know. I made plans on Wednesday . . . Oh, Jimmie, no. I can't just cancel them, they're good friends. Good-bye."

This time it's not necessary for Celeste to add, "I wish you'd told me earlier in the week." Such an assertion was appropriate in the past when Celeste canceled her plans and left others hanging to stay in the good graces of her own children—as if they'd dismiss her from their lives if she didn't come through. But now it's as clear as brand-new skywriting that if they'd given her notice, told her on Monday as soon as they realized they'd need her, Celeste surely would have been there for them.

This is the way to create a crisis—a situation in which *the other person* is on the spot. You may have to do this repeatedly for him to treat you differently, and in the process teach himself to perceive you differently. It won't be simply your behavior but *his new treatment of you* that will change his view of you. In the case we've just seen, better treatment by Celeste's son will restore his appreciation of her real status.

By posing a crisis for the other person—inducing him to start another kind of projection on you—you may be creating a crisis in your own life too. You may well go through a period of wondering whether you're worth the upset to the other person, whether he—in Celeste's case, her own son—really loves you enough to forgive you for any inconvenience he may blame on you.

Much of this will be in your own mind. Of course, when you reverse your style so late in a relationship, you surprise people. They may react badly. Celeste's son might insist, complain, perhaps even accuse her of sabotaging his weekend. But, if forced to, he will find the ingenuity to solve his problems through other means. Obviously, his mother has the right to make plans too.

Even the most selfish of people submit to reality in its harshest forms, which often constitute much worse indignities than having a request denied. Celeste's son would have to stay home if there were a blackout or if his wife suddenly got an acute headache. And he will have to bear much greater defeats, those losses incident to life itself, such as advancing age and decrepitude. He'll either go ahead heroically or not; that's up to him. Either way, he'll surely recover from her having made plans of her own for Friday night unless he chooses to punish her by not recovering.

The method of creating a crisis always begins with the recognition of someone's pattern of inappropriate expectations of you, and your decision to stop acquiescing. In the past, you've done what the person expected and unwittingly playing into his Projection for some time. However, more recently you've protested, asking the person to stop, making your case as best you could—all to no avail. Now, you are taking a stand; you've chosen grounds for your decision that are above reproach. Making sure you're on firm ground is crucial if the other person is to feel the impact and see where he's at fault.

In addition it's important that you know, during the inevitable period of self-doubt, that the position you took is fair.

This requires that you not pick a vital moment in the person's life to break your pattern. Say a person you work with thinks of you as manipulable, answers questions directed to you, tells you what to say and to whom. If you've been going along with all of this, it's not fair to choose a moment critical to his career to throw him off balance. Your aim is to make your point and cease being an accomplice; your purpose is not revenge, but clarification of who you are. Again, limit yourself to the step you are taking. You are going to have your way this time. That is enough. No accusations or recriminations; simply do what you must.

7. *Altering or ending a relationship*

Finally, if all else fails, you may have to threaten to end the relationship, or at least to change its basis permanently. The *other person* is actually ending it by refusing to hear you.

There are people who may like you, or even love you, but who perceive you and treat you in a way that's utterly intolerable. You may have to warn such a person, "Unless you change toward me, we will be on a different basis." And that different basis may be total separation.

Of course, if the person is an intimate, this will be a desperate last resort. In most cases, you won't want to disown a son or daughter or a parent just because the person's Projection on you is utterly wrong. But even then, if the abuse is extreme, and if you feel that the person's perception of you is unchangeable, you may have to do this. Ideally, you'll leave open some route of access to you in the event the person comes to his senses.

Unfortunately, we've all had the experience of having to end a relationship that was once precious to us because we had simply lost all status with the other person.

In most cases, though, you'll be saved from this last dire stage if you act early—and decisively.

HOW CONSONANCE
WORKS IN YOUR FAVOR
──

One of the incredibly good things about using the Projection Principle is that when you head off even *some* harmful behavior and force a revision, *the other person will on his own augment his new, better treatment of you.* He will add actions of his own creation, some of which you won't even know about, to the new treatment that you've requested. Instead of enlarging his wrong image of you, he will enlarge his correct one.

AXIOM XIV: The principle of consonance says that when a person revises for the better *some* behavior towards you at your request, he will *on his own* change other behavior to be consistent with the improvements he's already made. He will align himself behind a new and better view of you.

SUMMARY
──

You now have a seven-step strategy for eliminating Projections that could prove harmful or fatal to relationships. Remember, the fewer of the seven steps you have to use, the better. As soon as you get the treatment you desire, *stop.* Your aim is not to express pent-up indignation, get revenge, or analyze the other person; it is simply to get better treatment as a route to being seen in the way you deserve.

Maintain a light touch wherever you can because even a slight intervention if undertaken early enough can be effective. No one else may ever know what you've done, but you will have stopped an avalanche of bad attitudes toward you from crushing a relationship by restoring a single pebble to its proper place before it is too late.

In some cases, you will need to describe the "better" or even seemingly "worse" treatment that you want. You may want to give reasons, particularly if it's someone close to you. In many cases, you'll have to deal with one or more of the five forms of resistance: *reality, humor, oversensitivity, ignorance,* or *emotional collapse.*

In the worst-case scenario, the person just won't change. Maybe you've touched a chord—a deep psychological need—with your request, and the person becomes irrational. You may need to create a crisis to get his attention, and if that proves insufficient, you may have to issue an ultimatum or even consider suspending the relationship or ending it entirely.

But these extreme measures will seldom prove necessary. If you are successful even to a small degree in getting someone to treat you better, their innate sense of consonance will induce them to continue to do so and to see you as you wish.

5

HOW CAN YOU KEEP PEOPLE SEEING YOU AT YOUR BEST –OR BETTER?

—

In a nineteenth-century French play *Le Voyage de Monsieur Perrichon,* two young men both want to marry the same woman, Henriette. They must compete, as was the custom, not for her love but for her father's permission to marry her. The father, Monsieur Perrichon, is a pompous bourgeois gentleman who has made his fortune very recently and now devotes his life to appearing cultured and well-traveled.

As the play opens, the two suitors, Daniel and Armand, meet by accident at a railway station. Each has discovered on his own that Perrichon is taking his wife and Henriette by rail to a ski resort for the week. So both have privately arranged to be on the train headed for the same resort, each of them hoping to beguile Perrichon into choosing him for a son-in-law.

As with all serious rivals for the same prize, Daniel and Armand are united in a sort of camaraderie by their similarity of purpose. They willingly reveal their strategies to each other. And no two strategies could be more diametrically opposed. Armand's is to make himself available to Perrichon, to satisfy his wishes—to do whatever he can to make Perrichon appreciative and a friend. Daniel's is to appear needy and get Perrichon *to do things for him.*

Daniel's strategy gives him the advantage. As Perrichon does good deeds for the youth, Perrichon savors his own power and comes to like himself greatly in the presence of this shrewd contriver. Daniel expertly creates needs that Perrichon can satisfy, gaps that Perrichon can fill, and as Perrichon does more and more for the youth, he favors him increasingly.

The game is almost won. For his coup de grâce Daniel arranges his most elaborate plot—it is Machiavellian in its understanding of human nature. Perrichon, who can hardly make his way on skis, even after lessons, has nonetheless scheduled an outing on Mont Blanc. Daniel positions himself along the route, ostensibly trapped in a crevasse and sure to die unless the noble Monsieur Perrichon comes along to save him.

It works. Perrichon rescues the youth. Flushed with success and imagining himself a hero, he instantly chooses Daniel for his son-in-law. How could he possibly resist the temptation to bring into his family a potential lifetime witness to his valor! But by a quirk of fate he overhears Daniel boasting of his clever scheme and changes his mind, and the audience goes home imagining that the better man has won Henriette's hand. But this last-act triumph of honest Armand over designing Daniel is an evident theatrical device; the message of the play remains with us.

This play by Eugene Labiche, who had over a hundred of his comedies and farces produced, is considered his best. It was a smash hit in 1860, and is still a perennial classroom favorite.

Labiche was a superb psychologist as well as a prolific playwright, and in this play he fastened on to a major truth. *The message of the play is that people will esteem us and project qualities onto us in accordance with how they treat us. To encourage the best possible views of us, it is not enough to deserve them: We must allow people, even encourage them, to treat us in ways that induce them to love themselves.*

The playwright anticipated that his audience would not accept Daniel's victory because Daniel's game plan seemed unnatural and full of trickery, as opposed to Armand's direct approach. But Armand's strategy wasn't really any more noble; his aim in serving Perrichon was to *obligate* him, or worse yet, to bribe him into handing over his daughter. By the standards of honesty and directness, Armand might have been disqualified as well as Daniel. Daniel's only sin was that his plan showed a better understanding of human nature. It was more deeply rooted in the forces that truly motivate people to make choices and act. For that reason, it was more compelling.

INDUCING OTHERS TO FLOURISH IN OUR PRESENCE

AXIOM XV: People must like themselves in our presence if they are to see us in a favorable light in the long run.

We may impress people with an unending list of desirable traits. But how they feel about themselves in our company dictates whether they will want us in their lives.

You've probably had the experience of going out with a potential lover who seemed to have everything. Man or woman, the person was charming, intelligent, rich, and seemed to have a glow of excellence. You were excited at first. It seemed as if crowds would part to make way for this person and, if you were lucky enough to be along, they would part for you too. On the first date, you felt unworthy and hoped the person would want to see you again. You were delighted when another evening was set up and hoped that you'd lose your stage fright. But by the third date things were, if anything, worse. You still felt that you had worn the wrong clothes, that your friends were mediocre and did you discredit; you wished you'd traveled more so you'd appear more cosmopolitan. Maybe you had sex with the person to bridge the gap and you felt ungainly and unsatisfactory. By the sixth date, you began to realize that you would always be uncomfortable with this person. It's not a matter of who *he* is; it's a matter of how *you* feel in his presence. And the simple truth is, you don't like yourself one bit.

You might ask Why? What am I doing wrong? Probably nothing. Then you realize that though his anecdotes are good, he doesn't encourage you to tell yours. You get a vague sense that you're not his type, that he's settling for you. You decide, courageously, that you're not happy with this person. You end the relationship. The key was that you didn't like yourself in that person's company.

How much better it would be to go out with someone not so attractive or accomplished, but in whose presence you feel wonderful about yourself. There are people who dedicate themselves utterly to becoming the perfect package, giving no thought at all to whether others like *themselves* in their presence. They sustain few friendships, if any.

From your own standpoint, always consider how well

others are able to like themselves when they are with you. One of Shakespeare's most beloved characters, and apparently a favorite of Queen Elizabeth I, was Sir John Falstaff, who bragged, "I am not only witty in myself, but the cause that wit is in other men."

Falstaff was for a long time the closest friend of the prince who later became King Henry V, and for good reason: an ideal quality for encouraging friendship is that of bringing out the best in others. The person who likes himself in your company will see you in the best possible light. He may not even be sure why he's promoting you over others at the office, or why he's inviting you to his country house for the weekend, or why he's asking you to marry him.

The art of reputation, of being liked and loved, must include the talent of enabling others to be at their best with us. *We have seen one of the essential ways of doing this in the story of Daniel and Armand: have the other person do things for you!*

AXIOM XVI: Allowing others *to do things for you* is crucial if they are to esteem you.

How many of us forget this and instead devote ourselves to doing things for others without letting them reciprocate! By insisting on such an imbalance, we unwittingly stop the growth of others' ability to care for us.

The key here is having the strength to show vulnerability. There are times when you need help with something, or you just need to talk to somebody. It may cross your mind that you don't want to burden the other person or be presumptuous. Or maybe you don't want to appear incompetent or needy. But it's not merely a matter of getting the help you sorely need at the time. You are also encouraging other people to contribute to your well-being. Each act of theirs on your behalf further convinces them that you are important to them, and worthwhile in general. Remember that their actions are constantly sending messages to their own minds.

Especially as parents, but also as lovers and as friends, we must remember to let people do things for us and express themselves at their best in order to encourage positive Projections. It is in large part by doing things for us that people convince themselves that we are precious in their lives.

It follows that we should never interfere when someone has established a healthy pattern of expressing care and concern for us by certain actions.

AXIOM XVII: Don't stop people from acts of kindness toward you. By such acts, the other person develops and sustains his good feelings toward you.

We don't mean to imply that you should take advantage of people or encourage them to make unreasonable sacrifices. But you *should* accept reasonable support that is freely given.

Harold, who is not very good-looking, doubts that Allegra, a lovely dancer, will want him for himself. In an attempt to interest her, he unwittingly uses money in a way that destroys any chance of developing a healthy relationship. Harold takes Allegra out in style: to a sumptuous dinner at his club and to the opera. The next week, it's dinner and a jazz cruise, and after he returns from a business trip, he takes her to a swank art benefit and auction. His generosity is attractive, but Allegra is beginning to feel a bit overwhelmed.

She decides that when Harold calls again, she'll be the one to do something for him. She doesn't make much money, but she's an innovative and exciting cook. She suggests preparing dinner for *him,* in her apartment, a gesture she can easily afford.

But Harold, fearing that Allegra won't like him if he takes too much, hesitates. He doesn't refuse outright, but he brings expensive flowers and champagne to her apartment. After dinner he suggests that they have a nightcap at an exclusive little spot that he knows well. He thus weakens the evening she has planned, depriving her of the chance to do something nice just for him and vitiating her generosity.

Allegra consents, but later realizes that Harold has trivialized her contribution to the pleasure of the evening. To have been the principal architect of a perfect evening for him might have helped balance the relationship, and Harold's acceptance of her offering would very likely have endeared him to her. But now that chance is gone.

The next week when Allegra turns him down, Harold is astonished. He thinks of her as an ingrate, but entertains the thought that for all his efforts, he simply wasn't handsome enough for her.

The following month he learns that she's going out with someone quite poor and that she has even split the cost of a vacation with that fellow, fifty–fifty. Now Harold rationalizes that Allegra just doesn't know which side her bread is buttered on. But in *giving* to the other fellow, Allegra is projecting onto him many desirable traits—humanity, similarity to herself, and even vulnerability. In the process she is now affording herself a sense of importance that she did not have with Harold, Mr. Takeover.

Refusing to accept what someone has to give, as Harold did with Allegra, is not the only way of interfering with a person's favorable view of us. In the following case, the person accepted the act fully, but *not* in the free spirit in which it was offered. As a result, she damaged a good relationship.

Faye, who runs her own ad agency, had a good relationship with Roger, her secretary; she had done favors for him, such as hiring his brother-in-law for temporary work, and advancing Roger a tidy sum of money when he needed it.

Roger genuinely liked her—for her decency but also because he himself had been allowed to make real contributions to Faye's welfare and to the advancement of the business. Roger's own pitching in with help beyond the call of duty had been critical in nurturing his devotion to Faye and in forming his Projection of her as "worthy of his best."

Then things changed. It was a Friday evening, and Roger was leaving for a two-week vacation in the Caribbean the following night. However, an emergency Saturday mailing needed to be done for a client, and two mailroom clerks got sick at the same time. Roger volunteered to work all day Saturday with Faye to get the mailing out, telling her he could make his plane if he left by six in the evening.

Normally, Faye would have accepted gratefully, though it would have been implicit that she couldn't afford to pay Roger for the extra work. But the firm had just picked up several new accounts and business was thriving so this time Faye offered to reimburse him.

"Thank you Faye, but that's really not necessary," Roger replied. "You've already done a lot for me."

But Faye insisted, virtually forcing the money on Roger, who reluctantly took it.

The next time an emergency arose, he couldn't help but know that if he volunteered, she would insist on reimbursing him. He hesitated to help her, but did. And, despite his misgivings about being paid, when once again she offered him money, he took it, reasoning that he had a family of his own to support.

True, Faye hadn't stopped him from engaging in his former behavior. But by paying him, she altered his *reason* for helping her. Formerly he did it with a high purpose, and it ennobled her in his mind. Now he was doing it at least in part for money. Having disturbed a Projection in which she was ennobled, Faye weakened Roger's view of her as a highly worthy person.

Sure enough, after a while Roger came to like Faye less, to respect her less. He thought, "If she has so much money, why doesn't she give me more?" Their relationship had changed.

And by the way, behind such a reluctance to accept payment as Roger's initial hesitancy, apart from hurt feelings, there often lies an unarticulated but accurate recognition that "something basic will change in our relationship if I am paid for this."

In this case, Faye interfered with Roger's freely given kindness, not by stopping an activity but by tampering with its motive. She stifled his urge to be a Sir Galahad, helping her out with her growing business.

Stopping people altogether from doing things for us is a hazard. But in the example of Faye and Roger, we see a second hazard: polluting the *meaning* of "kindness."

It's not enough to encourage behavior that causes others to see us favorably; we must be careful not to introduce *new motives* for *old behavior*—motives that would change the projective property of that behavior.

AXIOM XVIII: If someone is already good to you, don't bribe him in new ways. When the wheel is spinning, let it spin.

Those who have high self-esteem to begin with are the most likely to encourage favorable views of themselves and to discourage undesirable ones. They can accept compliments and recognize abuse.

On the other hand, those who *feel* undeserving, who can't possibly picture others liking them or doing things for them without ulterior motives, are liable to stop people when they do reach out. Faye, who insisted on reimbursing her secretary might have been in that category. It's easy to imagine, for instance, that if Faye had almost no background in her field before succeeding and felt slightly undeserving of her success, she might find it hard to let others serve her beyond their absolute requirements.

Harold—Mr. Takeover—whom we mentioned earlier, was in his middle fifties and prosperous. He went out only with women very much younger than he was because, he reported, they were the only ones who aroused him sexually. Like many such men, he refused to see this selectivity as a mark of decline in his capability for ready sexual arousal, preferring to construe it as a refinement of taste. He felt deeply unworthy of the women he wanted and unattractive to them. It was his own sense of unworthiness that motivated his "extras" whenever he did manage to attract a woman in his preferred age range. And those same extras destroyed her chance of caring for him and thus defeated him.

STAVING
OFF CONTEMPT
—

Since you want to be seen at your best, you must avoid two practices that invite others to see you in the *worst* possible way. Instinct may have given you a natural aversion to these habits of behavior, or your own experiences may have trained you out of them. But like other bad habits, these two behaviors can feel good at the time, which makes them dangerous and addictive. Your understanding of how projection works will show *why* they can do you in.

First, try to avoid making requests that another person almost surely won't grant. Some people constantly ask for outrageous things on the grounds that "there's nothing to lose." They convince themselves that repetition will pressure someone to give in eventually. With each refusal by the other person, they think they're getting closer to the inevitable yes.

What they don't weigh is the effect that refusing them has on the other person. Every time the person says no, he is adding to his picture of them in his mind as "someone to be refused." They have lost so much status by their ungrantable requests that further rejection of them now becomes natural. They have set themselves up to be diminished.

Barbara started a new job as a buyer at a department store in January. Immediately she asked for "flexible hours," but she was turned down because *no one* got them. A month later, she asked again and was again turned down. She was slow to learn the store's accounting system, so she asked her boss if she could be exempted from the calculative side of the job for a while. Her boss refused. Next, she asked for a bigger office with more light even though only two people out of twelve in the department had such offices and one of them was the boss herself.

The boss replied that offices went with seniority and again said no. Then Barbara announced that she was pregnant and asked to leave at noon on Wednesday because she and her husband were taking a course in the Lamaze Method. Again the boss refused.

In July Barbara took a four-month maternity leave. She'd been back at work for about a month by Christmas. Her Christmas bonus, which in this company was based on merit, was small. Barbara decided to complain to her boss yet again, and ask for an increase. It seemed to her that the worst she had to fear was being refused. But she was wrong. A month later, she was fired.

It wasn't that Barbara's work was so poor. Several other employees, no more effective on the job, received minimal raises in January and survived. And it certainly wasn't the maternity leave she took that cost her the job. What did her in was the boss's belittling view of her, the Projection that Barbara herself had fed, that of being "someone to be denied, a pain in the neck."

The boss had gradually created this Projection by the act of refusing her over and over again. The boss's recognition of Barbara's unsatisfactory performance, coupled with her need to say no so often, led her to conclude that Barbara had to go.

AXIOM XIX: Avoid putting people in a position of having to say no or to reject you. The other person's doing so persuades him even further that you are a person to reject.

Of course, we all face *some* rejections; we have people say no to us. In fact, the most courageous of us are those who push against the limits of what seems "usual" or "permissible"—nothing ventured, nothing gained. But the axiom is true nonetheless. It's a matter of assessing the likelihood of rejection, and using common sense. What's important is to understand the implications of being rejected, to consider your requests carefully, and to avoid creating a pattern.

Sensitive people know that this even applies to overstaying your visit in someone's home. The best guest will leave before the host crystallizes in his mind the desire to end the evening. Rather than forcing the host to yawn or talk about what an early day he has coming up or, in the worst case, to actually *ask* him to leave, the guest will depart voluntarily, leaving the host a little hungry to see him again. By scrupulously avoiding any sort of rejection at the evening's end, the guest is fostering his host's view of him as pleasant to have around, no trouble at all, and even a bit "scarce" and therefore desirable.

The other behavior to avoid if we wish to be seen at our best is any action calculated to evoke pity in another person. It may be tempting to tell the boss that he misrepresented the job and that he's been taking advantage of you for the last year. You might feel great for a moment to see your parents or your spouse weep at their mistreatment of you and what you've endured at their hands. Evoking pity in another is usually done with the aim of making the other person see how deeply and extensively he has hurt you so that he will be shamed into changing and giving you even *more* than your due—retroactive reparations.

But the technique backfires. The *real* monster will be unmoved; he won't even understand what you're talking about, and if he *does* catch a glimpse of the truth, he would rather walk away from you than take the trouble to change. The average person will not want to *see* himself as an ogre. Since he's capable of sympathy, he may understand that you've suffered. But not wanting to see himself as unreasonable or erratic, and perhaps not wanting to feel your pain, he will take measures to convince himself that he had good reasons for whatever he did—that you deserved it. He will justify his treatment of you any way he can.

"I don't how you can complain about still being in the stockroom. You've never shown any ambition until now!"

"Of course I shout at you all the time. Why should I stop? You don't understand anything else!"

In each instance, the self-pitying way you presented your demand caused the other person to consolidate his position against you. Had you approached him in a way that was less dramatic and that contained less accusation—had you left him some "out"—he might have acceded, or at least given your request some thought.

It's human nature to like those we've already treated well and to despise those we've already mistreated. Henry Ford once said, "A man will never forgive you for the wrongs he has done to you."

Whenever you position yourself as pitiable, you look like a loser. Since people have a need to picture a just world rather than an unjust one, they are instantly prompted to find things wrong with a loser that will explain why he's faring so badly. To preserve their Projection of a "fair world," they will indict the loser in their own minds.

If you have implied that the other person *himself* is to blame for your losing out in life, he will try even harder to explain his behavior as just treatment of you, and to convince himself that you deserved it.

Try to discipline yourself to keep your request as relevant as you can. Ask for what you need, but be assiduous about leaving out excess baggage: how you feel about not having the thing, what not having it has cost you, why you need it, or comments about how much better off others are who have it.

For example, Donna says to her husband, "Vinnie, you're not giving me enough money to run the house, we're putting too much into our savings. Just because I decided to have a baby and haven't worked for a year doesn't mean I shouldn't have any nice clothes any more. You wanted the baby as much as I did. And why should I have to scour for bargains at the supermarket? Edith doesn't, and she's had two children and hasn't worked for ten years."

Even if the request is fair and Vinnie would see this under ordinary circumstances, he's likely to feel so abused by the comparisons and hurt by the complaints that he'll unplug his hearing device. Donna's plea for pity is an accusation that Vinnie is making her life intolerable, and that he's doing so by being callous or cheap. In reaction, Vinnie is apt to take a negative stand just to preserve a vestige of dignity. If he does that, Donna has actually gone backwards by her presentation. Her issue is one that should have been discussed by equals in a marriage. *She* was the one who cast herself as an inferior, assigning him the part of withholding parent.

Donna hurt herself by overloading her request, by trying to induce Vinnie to pity her as a means of getting what she wanted, employing a method that may have worked for her since childhood when nothing else seemed persuasive. She would have done far better justice to herself if she had said something like, "Darling, let's sit down after dinner and go over the budget. There are some things I want, and I'd like to check into what we can afford."

Using pity as a device is a mistake commonly made on the job. The employee who uses suffering as an argument is sure to lose out later.

Nathan says he needs a bigger office because he's been in the firm for fifteen years and people laugh at his little cubbyhole. Estelle says she needs a promotion because her husband left her. Gene says he needs more money because his kids are entering college and his salary just isn't good enough.

If people are laughing at you, if your husband left you, or even if you haven't been organized enough to put away money for your children's education, you may be pitiable, but you also look threadbare in one way or another. Though the boss may give you what you ask for, he debits you subconsciously. He may not even realize himself why he doesn't regard you as a big winner. But inherent in your plea for pity is the statement that you're a loser, and an unashamed loser at that. You've led the boss to wonder why you've fared so badly. "Why *is* Nathan laughable?" "Why would Estelle want to go around announcing that her husband abandoned her? Doesn't she have any pride?" "Why would Gene fail to plan for his kids' future? Maybe he's really irresponsible!" Each of these people might have been warranted in making the request that they did, but not in construing themselves as tragic figures. In each case, the boss is invited to form a Projection of the employee as "below average."

Nathan should have restricted his argument to that of entitlement: "I'm senior in my department now, and this space just isn't adequate for the flow of people who come through here."

Estelle should have requested a promotion based on merit. She might have written a memo listing her accomplishments in the previous year, or simply discussed with the boss her ideas for future contributions to the firm, leaving out any reference to her personal life.

Either Gene had a case for more money based on job performance or he didn't. If he had a case, he should have presented it to his boss. If not, he should have considered other options such as improving his performance or seeking more money elsewhere.

The use of pity as a ploy is nearly always a throwback to the child-parent relationship. For that reason, it is extremely unromantic. Stan says to Madeline, whom he loves, "Can't I come over tonight? I know you're trying to work, but I'm so lonely."

If he succeeds at coming across as a needy child, Madeline may invite him over, but for Stan it will be the beginning of the end. Madeline now sees him not as a lover or an attractive sexual partner but as a kid she is burdened by. Indeed, it would be far better for Stan's position with Madeline in the long run if she turned him down, in effect refusing to see him as pitiable. Although he might feel uncomfortable alone in his own home for the evening, it's possible Madeline will mercifully forget his phone call and his ugly portrayal of himself.

Since it was ten o'clock in the evening, Stan should have fought to contain himself and not call Madeline at all. When he did call, he should have kept it brief and light. The minute Stan realized that Madeline was still busy, he should have gotten off the phone and given her back her evening.

AXIOM XX: Avoid evoking pity in others. Those who pity you will always disdain you as well. They will develop or nurture a Projection of you as "a loser" and will treat you accordingly.

ERRING AGAINST THE STEREOTYPE

Whoever you are, something about you marks you as a certain "type," who suffers a prejudice somewhere. You're young or old or middle-aged; you're a woman or a man; you're clearly ethnic or clearly not; you're heterosexual or homosexual; you're undereducated or overeducated . . . You are sure to suffer some Projections owing to a stereotype.

For instance, one of the stereotypes about women is that they're always late, another is that they're overly emotional. Any error of performance on your part that is consistent with the stereotype will hurt you twice as much as a random failing. Going *against* the stereotype, even to a slight fault, will hurt you least and may even help you. It's important to know which stereotype Projections you are subject to. Take special pains not to make the mistakes expected of you and, if anything, to overcompensate where a Projection against you already exists.

As a woman, be especially careful to get to work on time. Why should you allow yourself to be disqualified because of a trivial fault when you're excellent in every way at what you do? Be careful to remain composed during heated controversies at the office because what a man may see as "involvement" in another man he may see as "hysteria" in a woman.

If you're the oldest person in the office, nearing retirement, people may think that you're nonsexual, brittle, and senile. Don't complain that you're getting tired at three o'clock in the afternoon. Leave that to the younger crowd. Don't walk away when someone tells a joke with a sexual punchline. If you can't stand rock music and prefer classical, by all means say so. But remember that you felt the same way when you were twenty-two and swing was the alternative to Mozart. So don't blame your taste on your age.

This is not to say that you should hide your identity or avoid your "type," only that you should avoid the *misbehaviors* associated with the type—the kinds of behavior that you yourself would deplore. Certainly anyone has a right to gesture with his hands, anyone has a right to discuss the fact that he's gone back to school to get his high school diploma. Only be aware some people have ready-made ammunition in the form of prejudices and are more than ready to see you as still another representative, with the attendant negative traits, of your type: a "brutal, insensitive man," an "unfeeling Wasp," a "money-hungry yuppie."

AXIOM XXI: Everyone faces stereotypic Projections. Though you can't destroy all prejudice, remember that faults of yours consistent with the stereotype will hurt you most. Avoid playing into such ready-made Projections.

REINFORCEMENT
———

Because other people have a need to remain consistent, we should always let them know that they have been treating us well, when indeed they have.

The most successful people are often among the freest in expressing appreciation for others' contributions to their own accomplishments. While complainers incur anger and invite other people to find reasons why these "losers" deserved no better than they got, the appreciative folk invite others to repeat their former acts of kindness or generosity.

"Sam, I never would have become a partner in the firm without you. You gave me my first real opportunity, and I'll never forget that."

To which Sam is likely to reply, "Nonsense, Don; you deserved every bit of it. You would have succeeded with or without me. And anything else I can do for you, just let me know."

The same desire to perceive the world as just that motivates contempt for the self-pitier prompts people to applaud the person who does well in the world and who thanks others for helping him. Showing your appreciation invites others to view you favorably, because everyone wants to feel that when he does things for someone, it is for the *right* someone—someone who deserves assistance.

AXIOM XXII: Giving people a sense that they've been good to you when they have been motivates *more* good treatment.

Goethe wrote, "Appreciativeness is the highest form of civilization." Appreciativeness is also a key to being appreciated.

SUMMARY

People must like themselves in your presence if they are to see you in a favorable light. Their doing things for you is essential for them to develop a sense of your importance. Therefore, besides living up to your own standards and acquitting yourself well, encourage the other person's kindness toward you. To stifle another person's generosity is to stifle his favorable view of you.

Remember, it's important not to reimburse people too much for what they do for you: in effect you are robbing them of their chance to give you a gift freely and, in the process, form a picture of you as worthy.

It's also important to make others feel appreciated for the good treatment they *have* given you. Aside from the ethics of doing this, it motivates people to see you as deserving of their best and to give you more.

There are a few bad behavioral habits that stop others from treating you in ways that will cause them to see you in a good light. Avoid self-pity at all costs. Never imagine that getting someone to feel sorry for you helps your status in his mind. Also, avoid repeated requests that must be refused. Don't make yourself "a person to be turned down," or you will force others to justify their nay-saying and to like you less. When in doubt, err against whatever stereotypes you fall into. Don't give others a chance to develop ready-made Projections.

Nearly always, those who like themselves naturally tend to make others feel comfortable in their presence. They attract favorable views. Those with low self-esteem tolerate and dole out the very behavior that generates contempt for them in the minds of other people.

The management of other people's projections, discouraging bad pictures of you and enhancing good ones, is also a recipe for learning to respect yourself more.

6

HOW CAN YOU SPOT YOUR OWN PROJECTIONS?

—

If you've lived with three different lovers and each relationship ended when you discovered in shock that the person was having affairs behind your back, it's almost sure that you have a problem of Projection.

If you've hated your last seven bosses, you have a Projection problem, just as you do if you *liked* all seven, but *they* hated *you*.

If you're a woman and you distrust all men or you're a man and think all women are grasping, you have a Projection.

These are all extreme cases, ones in which you have been systematically blind to a reality.

Your Projection—your selective vision—dictates what is within and without your psychic range.

Certain qualities are readily discerned by those holding a very strong Projection. The person projecting can spot these qualities in others immediately, and will often attribute them where they don't exist. On the other hand, the same person will be almost totally unable to see certain other qualities, unless they are so obvious that no one could miss them.

Consider, for example, a man who lived with three different lovers and was disillusioned each time. He's clearly prone to project, but it could be in either of two ways. Perhaps in the course of a relationship, this man *acts* in ways that produce paranoia: he persuades himself that his lovers are betraying him and mocking him. He sees the quality of infidelity when it is there *and* when it isn't. He imagines she is unfaithful even when she is not. His projection of mistrust may actually encourage in his lover a tendency for her to be unfaithful, a behavior that she might not even considered with a less jealous or paranoid mate.

Or, the man may hold a Projection that is almost the opposite. It may be that he ordinarily sees women through rose-colored glasses: All of them appear honest, faithful, even ingenuous. With that bias it is hard to for him to conceive of a disloyal woman, and during the early part of a relationship, he may miss all the signals of impending unfaithfulness that another man without this bias would easily spot. Only when the evidence hits him on the head can he *see* infidelity and realize that he selected the wrong person.

As for a woman who hated her last seven bosses, it's conceivable that they were all hateful, but more likely, their bad qualities were in the eye of the beholder. The poet Alexander Pope said, "All things look yellow to the jaundiced eye." In this case, sheer numbers seem to inform against the woman, implying that when it comes to author-ity figures, she sees only *bad* qualities.

If she *liked* the bosses but they *hated* her, then it's obvious that her Projection caused her to *miss* things. The bosses may have disliked her for good reasons, reasons that the woman herself supplied by her persistent inability to see growing annoyance in another. Perhaps her Projection that her bosses were like permissive parents who would hold nothing against her gave her a latitude in her own mind that she had no right to take in reality. Each time she disappointed a boss, he would give up on her a little more. Not recognizing her diminishing position, she would continue in her ways until finally she would be called into his office and fired.

Such a seemingly benign Projection—that everyone is on your side, no matter what—can do you as much harm as seeing all the world as malevolent. You are unable to see even hatred. With this deficiency, you will make disastrous choices in many relationships.

On the grand scale, women who see *all* men as a stereo-type or men who see the same qualities in *all* women have wildly selective vision—they must be manufacturing much of what they see.

AXIOM XXIII: Your own Projections deter you from reading people the way you should. You can fail to see traits and qualities vital to relationships, and you can imagine that you are seeing traits and qualities that aren't really there.

Your own projections can cheat you out many of the good things in life. You might miss honesty, intelligence, or even love when it is offered. You can't enjoy what you can't see, and your Projections—your blind spots—delude you into feeling alone when others are really giving you what you want.

If you project "danger" onto the world, you might force yourself to remain isolated or pass up taking risks that could pay off in friendship or career.

In other cases, Projections amount to a denial of potential trouble, of bad intentions where they *do* exist. Those holding such Projections can be taken advantage of over and over again. Such people will trust the wrong business partner or marry the wrong mate. Someone seeing kindness and good intentions everywhere will fall prey to ill-wishers. The projector of insistent optimism won't know friends from enemies, and those who do the most for him will feel misunderstood and unappreciated.

AXIOM XXIV: To project a desirable trait onto a person or onto the world is to become blind to real dangers. To project an undesirable trait is to imagine dangers where they don't exist and to lose sight of potentials in relationships.

It may sound like a formidable task to stand outside of yourself and *identify your own systematic distortions.* To you, who live with them intimately, they don't appear as distortions but as reality. Dostoevsky said, "A person doesn't think he *thinks* a thing is so; he merely thinks it is so."

AXIOM XXV: One of the chief reasons that our own Projections seem so natural to us is that, ordinarily, we continue to act on them over a lifetime. With each action consonant with the Projection we further persuade ourselves that what we are seeing is really there.

However, there *are* devices you can use to find out if you're prone to "think" certain things are so, whether or not they are.

SIX WAYS TO SPOT
YOUR OWN PROJECTIONS
---

1. *Use the test of "universality"*

One way of spotting a projection is to apply the test of *universality.* If you see the world as unrelentingly one way, if it seems that everyone, or all women or all men, are out to take advantage of you, or that all people are stingy or generous, or that all people appreciate only success, or that all are disloyal, or that all are stupid or materialistic, or that *all people* are *anything* in particular, you are projecting.

Projections color your world view. You are likely to attribute your beliefs about people's true nature to the many conclusions you've drawn based on what you've observed over the years. But other people, living in the same world as you and having seen the same things, feel very differently about people's nature. Thus, your world view says more about your Projections than about the world.

Bob was a cynic. He was a political correspondent for a Washington-based weekly magazine. He seldom got a by-line because his stories were dull and unaffirmative and even his negative exposés lacked verve. On the rare occasions when he went out for dinner with friends or was invited to a party, he ceaselessly talked about corruption, about how rotten the political machine was, and about how all the concerned people are gone and everyone today has a vested interest. He was fond of saying, "Truth is only a pawn that people put on the square they want." Bob could not be described as "a real fun guy."

Bob liked to say that the management of his weekly, along with most of his colleagues, were morons. He also deprecated his wife's brother, a successful lawyer and a warm person. After a while her brother avoided him. Bob was cynical about his son's chances to make it as an accountant in Washington. "To get anywhere around here, you'll have to be a good crook like the rest of them," he said.

Finally Bob irritated his bosses into dumping him and was let go with minimal severance pay. The previous year, he'd embarrassed his wife, Nancy, into quitting her executive job at a government agency by constantly mocking her in public for working for "a bunch of inept, corrupt politicians." With Bob unemployed, Nancy instantly took a job at the local dry cleaner to make some money. However, Bob soon began making cynical remarks about the small contribution women can make when they work, and he even accused Nancy of not really wanting to work at all.

When he made this charge in front of friends at a dinner party, Nancy burst into tears. "What the hell do you *want* from people?" someone asked. "I don't know how they put up with you as long as they did at the magazine. *I* would have fired you years ago the way you run everyone down."

Soon after that Nancy left him.

Within months he began to miss her terribly, and he did some soul-searching. *"Am* I a cynic, someone incapable of appreciating honest effort?"

Instinctively, Bob applied the test of universality, perhaps getting the idea from the many remarks made to him throughout his life that nothing ever satisfied him, that no one seemed to be trying. If he couldn't see good intentions or capabilities *anywhere,* then the problem must be in *the way he perceived.* Using the universality test, he had identified a Projection of his, one that had almost destroyed his life. Fortunately for him, Nancy took him back on the condition that he go for therapy to work on his outlook, which he did manage to change.

Often it takes a crisis to jar someone into awareness of a

bias. You might think that seeing the world—or all mothers, or all men—in a certain shade of gray is not a distortion, but it is.

Ask yourself, "Do I have an unvarying belief about bosses, or employees, or older people, or wives, or children, or human nature itself?" If you do, you are surely projecting because there is infinite variety within even the smallest category.

2. *Look for a feeling or judgment conspicuous by its absence*

Eleanor, who is now in her late fifties, never finished high school, but for more than thirty years has run the circulation desk at a prestigious medical library. She breaks her neck working overtime and is utterly unappreciated—hardly even noticed by the doctors, few of whom know her name. Every evening, Eleanor tells her husband, Harry, stories of incredible feats of healing by this and that doctor, following each one's career as though he were a personal friend. She savors the offhand comments doctors have made to her while she served them, feeling ennobled by their status, and she expects Harry to share her reverence. But he is a garage mechanic and has had less noble experiences with physicians, many of whom demand that he drop everything to fix their cars first, and then rarely tip and hardly ever say "thank you."

Eleanor's projection of greatness on doctors and on educated people in general eclipses her husband and herself. How can she spot and destroy this Projection so that she can see herself and Harry as being on a level with any decent, hardworking person? She might look for what is conspicuously *absent* in her feelings when with doctors and in her judgments about individual doctors. She's *never* lost her temper with a doctor. She's *never* felt a doctor to be culpable of any sort of negligence or poor performance. She's *never* held up to question any aspect of a doctor's personal life. In fact, she's *never* even been bored by a doctor.

Clearly, Eleanor is unable to see any shortcoming or even human failing in a physician. Such a suspension of judgment bespeaks a Projection.

In another example, Peter has been married for twenty-four years to a to semi-alcoholic, spoiled woman, who is full of diatribes on how to live and behave. He becomes involved in an extramarital affair with a hardworking, self-sufficient woman, Marianne, who appreciates his gifts and pays close attention to his needs. When his teenage son gets into trouble in school, Peter hesitates to discuss the problem with his wife, who is full of blame for him and his son, but finds Marianne sympathetic. She even helps him hunt down various resources to help the boy get back on his feet.

But Peter sees no fault in his wife's performance. He thinks of her as solid, proper, his authentic mate on this earth. He is incapable of recognizing Marianne's contribution—its inventiveness and its uniqueness. When he takes a suggestion from Marianne, he later forgets that it's hers and automatically attributes it to his wife. When Marianne leaves work early on two afternoons to call and interview special tutors for his son, Peter is hardly even able to grasp what she has done for him.

Peter's projection on his wife is the one he applies to all wives and *certified spouses.* Thus, he insistently perceives his own wife as loyal and totally on his side. Were he to apply the test of what is conspicuously absent in his view of his wife and of wives generally, he would soon appreciate his incapacity to spot irresponsibility, lack of interest, and slovenliness about things that count.

On the other hand, what he cannot see in *mistresses* is devotion and intelligence. He cannot imagine that he could have central importance in the life of a woman to whom he is not married or that he could be unique and irreplaceable to her. By applying the test of what's missing, he might discover his two contrasting Projections: on "wife" and on "mistress."

In using the test of what's missing to spot a Projection, there are two good questions to ask yourself. The first is, "What traits do I virtually never see in others?" For instance, you might realize that you've never thought of anyone as "treacherous," or that you've never seen a man as "tender." Perhaps an extreme case of Projection was Will Rogers's comment "I never met a man I didn't like." If he really felt that way, he certainly didn't see much diversity in human nature.

The second question to ask yourself is, "Is there any particular feeling—anger, fear, pity, sympathy—that I've never had toward people in some category?" For instance, you've never been afraid of being cheated by a salesmen or of being misdiagnosed by a doctor. Or, you've never pitied a man who's been left by a woman because, "Men are tough and they can take it; it was probably his fault anyhow."

If you've never thought of anyone as "treacherous," and you've never feared being cheated or ill-used, you almost surely have a fixed Projection of the world as kindlier and less varied than it really is. The dangers are obvious. If you never see a man as "tender," or as capable of being torn apart by the loss of a lover, you are Projecting a toughness on men that is unfair to *them,* and which inhibits *you* from enjoying the softer side of them.

Here you are testing for Projections by asking, "Which qualities do I seldom or never see?"

3. *Study the mistakes you make over and over*
Whenever you see a pattern in your life of a certain kind of behavior that has caused you unhappiness many times, there's almost certainly a Projection attached to it.

Ask yourself why you engage in the behavior and you may realize that you're doing it because you harbor a false impression of people.

You've just gotten home from work on Friday, and you're looking forward to a quiet evening at home. You answer the phone thinking it's a friend whose long-distance call you are expecting, but it's your neighbor. She says she is having a bunch of people from the neighborhood over at nine-thirty. Will you come? Before you know what you are doing you answer yes. You slam the phone down hating yourself and resignedly set the VCR to record the movie you were dying to see that night.

Why do you always do this? It's the fourth time recently that you've given in to something you didn't want to do. It's getting to the point where you're afraid to pick up the phone because you can't say no to anyone who asks you for anything.

What do you think will happen if you don't agree to go to a football game you don't care about, or if you don't spend Saturday baking for a community fundraiser? Or if tonight you don't accept your neighbor's invitation to visit?

Ask yourself *exactly* what you fear, and you will be led directly to your Projection. Maybe you fear the other person will *hate* you for refusing and never speak to you again. You may further fear that she will tell others you are uncooperative and not someone worth knowing. You may even go so far as to believe needlessly that refusing someone—almost anyone—will have reverberations on your career, your love life, your very security.

Clearly, your faulty impression—your Projection on people—is that they are utterly demanding and will tolerate no individual freedom or choice on your part, no deviation from what they expect of you. Moreover, you project that they are vengeful and will stop at nothing to destroy you if you cross them. Common sense may tell you that this is not so, and certainly, *you* are not like this yourself. But the Projection may have been with you for years; perhaps a parent warned you that people were brittle and that you'd better behave, or it might be that one of your parents was such an intolerant person.

Whether you have a pattern of hiring the wrong people or choosing the wrong jobs, whether you find yourself buying things that don't fit or are unable to buy anything for yourself at all—whatever the repeated pattern, the test applies.

Perhaps you are repeatedly disappointed in people or in yourself. Several different friends have betrayed you or dropped you abruptly when they moved up in social status. In retrospect, you see you have a pattern of trusting the wrong people. Or you are disappointed in yourself for repeatedly promising friends too much and then letting them down. You see that you play the "big shot" and discover your Projection: that people will like you only if you can deliver big things. In reality, people are quite willing to accept you as you are.

Always, where there is a habitual action, there is a habitual perception. Each feeds the other. When you question the action, you will usually be led to discover the Projection that is fed by it, and which in turn contributes to it.

4. *Use the method of magnification*

Let's say that you're constantly doing something you hate because you can't say no. But when you ask yourself *why* you can't or what you fear from the other person if you refuse him, nothing comes to mind. Studying your mistake—asking yourself why you continually harm yourself by some behavior—doesn't seem to point toward any Projection. You're just *afraid* to say no; you don't know why.

There is a method to heighten your understanding in a case like this so that you *can* catch a glimpse of your Projection: *Do the thing that's hard for you—even once, even falteringly. Your reaction to doing it will magnify your Projection. You will vividly see what you were afraid of or what bad outcome you expected.* Because you are magnifying your true fear or expectation, we call this the method of magnification.

Choose the one person in your life you really trust and whom you feel you can take a chance with. When this favorite person, say your sister, calls and asks you to go shopping with her in a store you loathe, take a deep breath and say no, just this once. Now, when you hang up, since you have a problem, you may be in a state of panic. Possibly you'll want to call back right away and say you've changed your mind, or even apologize for declining.

But don't! Instead, study your panic and ask yourself, "What does it seem to me she is thinking about me *right now?*" Thoughts may come to mind such as, "She despises me and will never forgive me"; or "She'll tell Mom that I let her down, that there's something wrong with me."

You've discovered the Projection. It might be that the other person will walk out on you, or collapse if you refuse him, or that he'll say nothing but tell everyone you're unreliable or even insane. The picture that comes to mind when you force yourself to go against *any* usual practice even once is a vivid magnification of your Projection. The method of magnification consists of breaking a pattern just once and studying the picture of the other person that comes to mind.

5. *Study limits in your own performance*

There may be certain things you just *never* do, though you realize that it would benefit you to do them. Perhaps close friends tell you that you should do them, and you know they're right. Or you see other people doing such things and reaping rewards.

You avoid sex with a particular person, though you really want it and just "know" it would be right for you. Or you've just started a small retail business but you've set your prices much too low. You know damn well customers are used to paying more, but you're afraid to charge them a fair price.

There's a limitation in what you're willing to do—in what you feel that you *can* do.

As you study your limitation, you'll usually be led to a Projection. For instance: "Richard will think less of me if I go to bed with him."

You didn't think that about other men you've had relationships with, but you're in love with Richard and your Projection of him is that he is a moral, high-minded, slightly delicate, easily offended gentleman.

Or, say you're the retailer: how come you don't charge the amount of money you deserve for your goods or services? Studying this limitation, you realize that you picture your customers walking out indignantly, saying to themselves, "She's not well enough established to charge as much as others do." It's a Projection, of course, that others have X-ray eyes and can see your own self-doubts and inexperience.

Many people holding a Projection of the world as "dangerous," for example, go through life failing to utilize great gifts of discernment, intelligence, creativity, even love, because they're afraid to take risks. They limit themselves because of their Projection and cede to others opportunities that are rightfully theirs. They don't stake their legitimate claims in the world. Often, when their friends exhort them to expand, saying, "You are worth so much more than you realize," they become stubbornly angry. They seem able to show great aggression toward their well-wishers, which would have served them far better had they used it on their own behalf to compete in the marketplace, or in love, or to demand the sort of treatment they deserve in any situation.

Were such a person to study her angry words when prodded by a well-meaning friend, she would be led right to the cause of her limitation—namely, her Projection. "You're crazy, I can't possibly charge that much for my flowers. People will *know* I just started, and they'll think I have some nerve being so greedy and pushy when I couldn't possibly know what I'm doing yet." The Projection that comes out in this argument is that people have X-ray eyes and ready disdain; that you live in a dangerous world, filled with people ready to crush you.

After you've studied a limitation, try to push against it, even once. This is another use of the method of magnification. The fears that come to mind will delineate your Projection even more vividly. Associated with every block, every emotional limitation to what you can do, is a Projection of some kind.

6. *Take stock of your strengths*

The last of the six ways to identify a Projection of yours is to study any *strength* you pride yourself on greatly.

This may seem surprising at first. Why investigate what's *best* about you when you're searching for a personal deficiency? But our strong points are likely to breed Projections.

For instance, Alex brought up his two younger brothers after both his parents died in a car crash when he was eighteen. He fought attempts to parcel out the family, proving that he could make a good living as an apprentice in a meat market. He had always had mechanical aptitude and after work did odd jobs for neighbors—building bookshelves, fixing pipes, even rewiring. At twenty, he left the butcher shop for a job in a hardware store, which he later bought and ran successfully. His customers thought him the embodiment of composure, confidence, and competence.

Alex remained fanatically independent, refusing any financial assistance from his aunts and uncles. Along the way, he was offered several jobs in businesses run by relatives but turned them down, seeing them as "charity." Both of his younger brothers won scholarships to college, but Alex asked them not to work even part time; he would buy their books and pay for their dormitory so they could devote themselves to study. His brothers told him all their problems and looked up to him, but he never "burdened" them with any of his.

When he was thirty-two Alex met Rita, the woman he wanted to marry. She considered him the strong, silent type but felt she hardly knew him. He did a lot for her and even helped her family redesign their home. Everyone thought Rita was incredibly lucky to have him, but Rita wasn't so sure.

In her view, he was a man of great strength. But she couldn't help feeling that allied with his strengths were parallel shortcomings. Alex would not express warmth, affection, or need for her. His need to be in control in all situations bordered on the obsessive, Rita felt diminished, unsure whether she had any real place in his life.

His independence, which had seen him through vicissitudes over the years, had also bred a terrible deficiency. Alex's Projection on others was that they would disqualify him if he showed even a hint of weakness. If he ever appeared childlike or fragile, if he let down his defenses with even one person, everything would be taken away from him.

Rita tried to prevail on Alex to open up more but met opposition. It wasn't easy for him to look critically at a trait that he had carefully developed and felt proud of.

Every strength you're proud of has taken precedence in your life. You have worked on it, had dreams about it, seen others in terms of it. You have depended on it, perhaps to the exclusion of other traits. You may well imagine yourself adrift without it, and inherent in that concept is a picture of other people *esteeming you mostly for that trait.*

If you pride yourself on your good looks, you're dangerously close to imagining that they are the key to your relationships. Your Projection is that people count on those good looks and might not cherish you if you lost them. The dangers of this kind of Projection are evident. For one thing, growing older will be especially hard.

If you want to know where you're apt to be projecting, ask yourself what you pride yourself on most.

Your strengths breed Projections because you almost surely see your successes as owing to those strengths into which you put such great effort. Each time you attribute another success to your treasured strength, you further persuade yourself of the Projection—that other people care desperately about that one trait of yours.

Whatever your strength is, there's a tendency to feel that without it you'd be lost. Buy an expensive new outfit for an interview, and you're likely to feel that it got you the job. Become known as expert on world events, and you'll imagine that friends come to your house for your insights. If you picture that your strength as a mother is protecting your children from all the things that can go wrong, then when they become adults and learn to fend for themselves, you'll imagine that you have absolutely no place in their lives. In each case, the strength breeds the Projection.

SUMMARY

Your own Projections set limits on your range of vision. They heighten your ability to see certain traits and blind you to others. They keep you from being the accurate reader of people that you will have to be if you are not to overlook love or friendship where they are offered or seek them where they are not.

Projections cheat you whether the qualities you imagine you see in other people are good traits or bad.

Because you have been acting consistently with your Projections over a lifetime, sustaining and reinforcing them by everything you've done, whatever you see appears very natural to you. That is why it is harder to spot your own Projections than anyone else's. If you're seeing the world through rose-colored glasses, how do you know you're wearing rose-colored glasses?

The challenge lies in stepping outside of yourself and observing your own way of perceiving. We have detailed six ways of doing this.

You may spot your own Projections by *applying the test of universality; searching for feelings conspicuously absent; finding Projections behind your own repeated mistakes; using the method of magnification; examining the limits of your own performance;* and *taking stock of your strengths and the Projections they breed.*

Spotting your own Projections is a prelude to changing them. You've seen in this chapter how, by changing even one routine habit, you can open the floodgates to a wave of discoveries about what you really think.

By changing a *set* of actions, you can give yourself a whole new vantage point on life. You can do what years of therapy might promise to do for you.

7

HOW CAN YOU CHANGE YOUR PROJECTIONS?

—

It's stunning to think that what you see may not really be there. In a curious way, it's often more seductive to hang onto a false picture of someone than to reconsider it. But though changing a Projection is not without its jolts to one's equilibrium, the reward is always worth it in the long run, just as the reward for breaking a self-destructive habit is always worth it.

A Projection is a mental habit, usually one supported by many behaviors. Once you've identified a Projection and set out to change it, expect all the inner repercussions that occur when you battle any habit—more in fact, since you're going to break a set of related habits, not just one, in order to change your outlook.

Russ's Projection is that of acute conventionality. For the last twenty years, he and his wife have been living a cold war. But it seems to him that everyone from his grown children to his co-workers would despise and disown him if he broke up his marriage, and that no one would talk to him if he lived alone. Maybe his wife would collapse and die and he'd be responsible. With such a view, it's no wonder he's dutifully stayed with her all these years, even turning down an affair with a woman he really wanted.

In reality, everyone feels sorry for Russ because they know he's suffering in a loveless marriage. His children would rejoice to see him happy, and his wife would hardly notice if he left. In fact, she'd relish having one more thing to complain about if Russ abandoned her. But Russ refuses to see this.

If he were to leave and discover it for himself, he would doubtless feel like a total idiot for having stayed so long. He would feel utterly foolish when he considered the sacrifices he'd made and how little he got in return. His Projection on his wife as fragile and needing him, when she didn't; his Projection on his colleagues as requiring him to be stationary and conventional; his Projection that his college-age kids would hate him if he left their mother, when they were primarily interested in his happiness; his Projection on marriage as a prison—all would become thunderously apparent to him. He would feel mocked by all these realizations that he had lived falsely. The shock of recognition would be tremendous.

It would take real courage for Russ to endure it.

Avoidance of this shock is a strong motivation for Russ to stay on his present path of life. By staying, he can avoid the anxiety of flying in the face of all his self-imposed taboos. He can avoid feeling mocked by a close reckoning of what he has already lost. He can go on believing that marriage, even if both parties are miserable, is the *only* way, that it's a lesser evil.

Being conventional, Russ has done what was expected of him almost from Day One. By now he's come close to forgetting what *he* really wants to do, which is how he got into this and other troubles in the first place.

This might seem like an extreme case in which a set of Projections govern a person's life completely. But the barriers that Russ would have to break to recover his life are, to some degree, those that confront anyone trying to change any habit.

Remember, a Projection is only a bad habit of mind, a habitual way of seeing people, that interferes with your life.

There's the illusion that the way you view people, how they appear to you, is set. You may say that, ever since you were a child, you've seen people in a particular way. You see people as fearful or tired or in a hurry or demanding or fragile or easily led or impossible to please. Whatever the view, it dates way back—*it is you.*

Because you've lived with your way of seeing people for such a long time, it's understandable that you feel you're stuck with it. It's tempting to conclude that everything you do springs from who you are—from that basic vision you've always had. It's tempting to believe that it would be impossible to change.

But what you do does not simply spring from who you are, it *creates* who you are. Your actions do not merely reflect your viewpoint; they *form* it.

AXIOM XXVI: Your actions are constantly *causing* you to see people the way you do, in the way you first learned to see them.

AXIOM XXVII: Every time you act in accordance with a Projection—even one you've held since childhood—

you *reinforce* that Projection; you sustain it. Without that constant sustenance, it would die.

Russ's parents were strict, hard-working immigrants, and he had to conform strictly when he was a child. His parents believed that the best way to survive in a new country was to keep your nose to the grindstone and maintain a low profile. Russ was told not to argue in public, never to question authority, not to make light of any civic ceremony like marriage or citizenship, and to let others go ahead of him in line if there was any question. He was told he had to live with his own mistakes, and he learned to take no risks. He did what he was told to do, feeling that he had little choice.

That was fine when he was a kid. It made sense if he wanted peace in the family, which he did. But it doesn't explain why now, at fifty, Russ still wants peace at any cost. There's plenty else he learned in childhood that he no longer believes. Why does he hold onto this?

The answer is that all through life Russ kept reinforcing his Projection that people demand conformity. He reinforced his Projection by conforming.

Russ's parents died by the time he was twenty-three. They weren't around to whisper in his ear that he should marry a girl of the same religion or from the same neighborhood instead of the woman he met when he was on vacation in Greece, whom he really loved. They didn't insist that he work as a bank executive instead of starting the real estate business he always dreamed of. They didn't tell him that, as an adult, you must stay with your wife even if you don't love her.

Russ did all those things on his own, in response to his Projection on the world. *And all those acts kept his early Projection going.* They renewed it.

Whenever Russ acted in a way that stemmed from his

desire to conform, he was reinforcing a bad habit, a bad habit of mind.

Your Projection, the way you've seen people perhaps since childhood, is a habit that needs actions to keep it going—*your actions.* It *can* be broken. You are not stuck with who you are and how you see the world.

AXIOM XXVIII: Because your every Projection is a habit of mind relying on actions for sustenance, the Projection can be broken if you stop the actions and replace them with other actions.

If Russ hadn't been trying so hard to conform, if he had "done his own thing," he would see the world as less restrictive and demanding.

By the way, all psychotherapy seeks to enable people to see themselves in positive new ways, to see the possibilities in the world and in other people—to alter Projections. The patient comes in with a fixed way of viewing himself and others. The only way anyone can change his view is by discontinuing the many activities that support that view and replacing them with new activities supporting a new and better picture of himself and others. Therapy succeeds to the extent that it helps people create a new view, and alter their Projections.

Few would care how they saw the world or themselves but for the fact that many wrong views result in great unhappiness.

However, by changing your *own* behavior, if you know precisely which actions to change, *you can do for yourself* much of what therapy purports to do and often does over time. You can change your own outlook and achieve what you've always wanted.

CHANGING YOUR OWN
PROJECTION: THE METHOD

1. *Pinpointing the projective behavior*

You felt uncomfortable about some aspect of your life—usually in your relationships with others or in your ability to function. You studied your outlook using the six identifying devices in the last chapter and you reached a remarkable conclusion: You are systematically off in the way you see people!

The next step is to discover how this improper world view leads you to act. *Ask what the Projection is motivating you to do. What do you do because of the Projection that others, without it, would not do?*

Joel secretly believes that he's the smartest person in the world. His Projection of people as stupid and unreliable is costly to him. How does he act on this projection?

Joel is successful in his field, which happens to be accounting. But he also imagines that he knows every other field better than even its specialists do. He makes a lot of independent judgments instead of consulting experts, and many of his decisions backfire. He doesn't listen very well, and he doesn't ask questions.

When he decides to rewire his recreation center, he declines help from a brother-in-law who's an electrician and does the job himself after a few hours of flipping through a do-it-yourself book. The lights blow. The wiring burns in the wall, and it costs Joel a small fortune to have several experts come in and repair his botched job. He has trouble listening even to them, and one of them bellows at him, "Don't tell *me* my business!" Joel tries to hide his failure from everyone. Later, he boasts that he did the job as efficiently as a pro could have.

In another case, Heather believed that her boss, Anne, wanted to crucify her and would never give her a chance to show her stuff. Heather's Projection was that all bosses are resentful, merciless people or they wouldn't get where they are. Based on this Projection, Heather acted in many strange ways.

Even before she'd *met* Anne, Heather began coping with a "merciless" boss. She lied about prior work experience in her résumé. Her first day on the job, Heather closely questioned other of Anne's employees on Anne's personal habits, preferences, and dislikes, on the assumption that special knowledge is always needed when dealing with an irrational person in power. As the weeks passed, Heather systematically hid her failures or blamed them on others, rather than let Anne "have anything" on her. She tried to ingratiate herself with Anne by telling her jokes and by publicly supporting Anne's policies even when she didn't agree with them; she made innuendos about colleagues, feeling that in so doing she was diverting Anne's inevitable wrath away from herself.

All this behavior of Heather's reinforced and intensified her terror of Anne and strengthened Heather's own feeling that she herself was in imminent danger. By acting on her Projection, she had convinced herself within a month that without such behavior, she would be fired.

These are just some of the activities associated with the Projections of Joel and Heather.

Joel and Heather pinpointed much of the behavior stemming from their particular Projections by asking themselves two questions. First, *"What does my Projection lead me to do that I would not otherwise do?"* Second, *"What do I do that is different from what others—those without such a Projection—would do in my place?"*

Clearly, if Joel had not projected stupidity on others, he would have asked for advice and heeded it, boasted less, listened more, and been willing to expose his mistakes like any other mortal.

If Heather had not seen all bosses as malevolent, she would have told the truth on her résumé, done her best on the job, and dispensed with all that research into what Anne was "really like." She would have dropped the various tricks she used to ingratiate herself and simply depended on Anne's honest appraisal of her work.

Joel's recreation-center wall would have been intact, and he'd have saved himself a lot of trouble and expense. Heather's job could have been fun instead of a paranoid torture.

In pinpointing the behaviors that you must change in order to change a Projection, *write down every behavior that the Projection is motivating.* Look carefully at others who do not hold the Projection, and see what they do differently, or don't do at all.

2. *Constructing a "ladder" for change*

You now have a list of activities associated with your Projection. You have a sense of what you must change if you are to see things differently, but you can't change everything at once. That would cause an incredible shock, and you'd probably become demoralized before giving yourself a real chance. You really wouldn't accomplish very much doing it that way.

Instead, order the behaviors in "rungs" of difficulty. Some of the projective actions you engage in will be relatively easy to stop; others, at the top of the ladder, may look impossible to change at this time.

For instance, take Russ, afraid to reconsider his bad marriage because of Opinion. His first step obviously could not be to leave his wife, saying, "I don't give a damn *what* anyone thinks." Even though he *knows* he has a Projection, he also knows that he still does give a damn—too much of a damn—about what people think, so this level of change just isn't emotionally possible for him right now.

But there are acts you engage in owing to the Projection, lesser acts, that you can dispense with at this stage. These acts represent the first rung of your ladder—the changes that are feasible right now.

Russ can stop telling everyone he has a happy marriage. He can stop acting shocked when others get divorced, and he can stop talking about divorced partners as "poor souls." There are other small acts of conformity in his daily life that he can drop. Such as shaving before going out to work in his own garden or wearing a tie to the office when he goes in on a Saturday.

Such changes will be the "easiest" because they will produce the least anxiety and terror. But he'll still be stunned at how hard it is to relinquish even these small habits, and at how uncomfortable he will feel initially.

On the second rung of the ladder will be changes that seem out of reach now, but that you can picture yourself making some day. When you are standing solidly on that first rung and doing effortlessly what you set out to do there, making the changes on the second rung *will* be feasible.

Russ will be able to talk to his mate about their incompatibility and maybe even work on the relationship and salvage it by facing the problem. Perhaps he was trying so hard to conform that he was even unable to say that there was anything wrong.

If the relationship just *isn't* salvageable, on that second rung might be the courage to reestablish friendships once precious to him that he had dropped at his mate's request. He might make freer judgments in his business, opting for the new over the traditional, opting for what he truly wants even though there might be risk involved.

On the third and highest rung of the ladder are the changes that don't seem even remotely possible right now. However, in the process of climbing the ladder, you yourself will have changed. You will see people differently, and the last set of changes, after you feel natural on the middle rung, will be no harder than the small improvements you've already made. By ascending the ladder, you change your vantage point and alter your own Projection somewhat, so that this final step won't be nearly as hard as it seems to you right now.

Notice that some revisions consist simply of *not* doing a thing. In other cases, it's a matter of doing something else *instead* of the thing you've always done.

For instance, Heather could replace her attempts at ingratiating herself, her bad-mouthing of fellow workers, and her character study of her boss by simply doing a better job in the time it took to do all that maneuvering.

The purpose of the ladder is to make it possible to scale the fortress on your own—to climb out from inside the self-made prison of your Projections. The more honest you are in setting it up, acknowledging what you can do right now, and what you can't, the easier your climb. If you try something too hard, too soon, you'll be tempted to quit altogether. But with each success, you're reducing the Projection just a little, and making your next step easier.

3. *Picturing yourself making the first changes*

You've constructed your ladder, and now you're contemplating the first change on the first rung. How do you feel?

Before the fact, the notion that you would be anxious about neglecting to shave before going to work in your own garden might seem ludicrous. "I'm not *that* much of a conformist," you might say.

But when the time actually comes to do it—*when you anticipate one of the first changes on your ladder*—you may feel a real twinge of anxiety. Your mind races as you consider the possible consequences:

"What if my boss drops over and I look like a slob?"

"What if my neighbor, Tom, sees me and thinks I've been up all night? What if he thinks I'm in some kind of trouble?"

"What if some real estate people come by and see me and think I'm poor and devalue the property?"

The more farfetched your answers, the more indicative that you are battling a real Projection. Use these thoughts prompted by anticipating the upcoming changes to put your finger on what you're really afraid of. You'll deprive this monster of some of its power if you can name it.

4. *Starting to change the behavior*

Now you're ready to start eliminating the Projection by changing the actions that spring from it and keep it going.

Some of these behaviors you'll be stopping entirely; others you'll be replacing with new behaviors.

You begin.

Whatever anxiety you felt when you anticipated the change was an *underestimate* of what you will now feel. With each change of a familiar behavior, you enter a no-man's land. You'll feel a strong impulse to retreat, to resume your old way of acting, which will appear sensible.

The first time Joel, who had always needed to see himself as the smartest man in the world and to see others as deficient, admitted a mistake, he felt panicked. It suddenly seemed to him that there was no way this could be a good strategy.

The first few times that Heather dealt with her boss directly, with no hidden agenda or defensive tactics, she expected to be fired. When Anne asked Heather what she thought of a new policy idea and Heather openly disagreed with what Anne had proposed, she felt sure that Anne would crush her afterwards.

These early reactions of chaos are real and very strong.

They are telling you that you're going against your perceptions, but this is no reason to stop.

Freud and the early psychoanalysts, who argued that nothing you do can change your way of seeing others, said that these reactions are insurmountable. But psychoanalysts subscribe to the theory that "you are who you are" inside, that everything you do springs from that core, and that you're stuck with it.

But, in reality, "who you are" is sustained by how you act. This is a truth you must cling to during this early period of uncertainty and discomfort. If you continue to battle against the distress and persist in your new actions, you will change "who you are." In fact, the anxiety itself is a signal that you're making headway, that you're changing.

5. *Free associating to the changes*

You can learn a lot about yourself and gain ammunition for further attacks on your Projection if you free associate at this stage.

Listen carefully to the voices in your head that are screaming, "Go back to your old behavior. It's natural. It's safe. It's correct." They'll back up their demand with dozens of reasons and elaborate justifications. In those excuses lies a picture of the other person, the one you're dealing with, or of the world as it's represented in one person.

By listening to those voices—and *interrogating* them—you will not only see your Projection in rich detail, but are likely to uncover where it came from.

When Heather disagreed with her boss at a meeting and shook with fear, she had to fight the voices that said, "Shut up! You'd better agree with Anne. Are you crazy?"

At home two hours later, Heather was still shaken. She asked herself, "Exactly what am I afraid will happen now?" She had a glimpse of the boss screaming at her in a raucous, high-pitched voice, slamming the table and pointing a finger. But that wasn't Anne's style at all. Anne was soft-spoken and very professional. Even in anger, she never raised her voice. Heather pushed on, interrogating herself further. "Why should Anne shout at me like that?" An answer came to mind: "She hates me for being young and pretty!" This too was ridiculous. Anne was no more than a few years older than she, and everyone said Anne was beautiful. Where had such a bizarre idea come from?

It took only a moment to figure it out. Heather could see her mother pointing that finger and screaming. Her mother always made derogatory comments about younger women, saying they could get away with anything, and was especially resentful of anyone pretty. She was demanding and unforgiving, always straddling the fence between tenuous acceptance and utter rejection of Heather.

The strategy for staying on her mother's good side that Heather had learned as a child was one she had sustained and added to over the years. She had used it with all authority figures—at camp, in college, and on jobs—and felt it kept her safe. Unknowingly, Heather had, by her own behavior, stamped "hysterical mother" on every boss.

And Joel, when he first frankly admitted a blunder to his brother-in-law, had the irrational picture of the man shrugging his shoulders in tragic disappointment.

Of course, that was not what happened. His brother-in-law just smiled genially and said, "We all make mistakes."

The reaction that Joel had expected was one that he had seen dozens of times in childhood. His father expected so much of all the children and was so easily disappointed that Joel had learned that only excellence, real or simulated, could get him through life.

Free associating about the other person when you change some projective behavior will often bring forth images that seem farfetched. *In a way, the more farfetched the images, the more you can learn.*

From these fragmentary images, you can piece together a complete picture of your Projection and even discover, in many cases, where it came from. This picture is your target. It is an illusion, a lie about another person or about the world that has been governing and diminishing you over the years.

And if you continue to study the illusion and the childhood figures behind it, you can learn even more. After Heather realized that she saw her mother in all authority figures, she began a mental search for other tactics she'd used with her real mother, tactics that were now a natural part of her repertoire with bosses. She realized that she had developed a false timidity to make her mother feel sorry for her, that she had assumed a slumping posture so as not to threaten her mother with her appearance. Early on she had acquired a saccharine smile. She resolved to eliminate all these mannerisms attendant on her Projection.

Joel recalled boasting to his father and promised himself that he'd stop exaggerating with others immediately.

All of this knowledge is ammunition. The more projective activities you can identify, the more effective you will be in eliminating them or replacing them in order of difficulty and in changing your Projection.

6. *Going up the ladder: coping with your fear of heights*
Each time you take a new step up the ladder, your feeling of strangeness, of wrongness in your new role will be renewed. Depending upon the nature of the Projection you're fighting, you may imagine initially that everyone is laughing at you or condemning you or preparing to take advantage of you or that people are fragile and easily offended and that you're overstepping your bounds. You'll feel anything from a pang of anxiety to mortification or stark terror.

Such distress may be much more acute than anything you felt over the years while you were reinforcing your Projection by routine self-defeating behavior. In those days, you may have lost lovers, friends, and jobs, been dissatisfied or disappointed with all your relationships, or even seen your life going down the drain. But from moment to moment you seldom felt this frightened.

Don't quit. The fear will go away if you stay on course.

At each new rung of the ladder you may wonder, "Why do I feel worse now, making a small change, than I did when I was seeing people in a very wrong way?" You may ask yourself, "Am I really doing the right thing? And if so, how could the right thing feel so wrong?"

The answer is that change is always harder than staying the same. Even change for the better feels unfamiliar—and curiously wrong. But don't give up.

You were like an overeater who didn't suffer while he was eating, but who looked in the mirror every morning and despised himself, afraid to approach a potential lover. Or like a smoker who enjoyed every puff, but fretted daily over the statistics and secretly worried about his worsening cough. *What you were doing felt fine, but the results felt awful.*

The overeater and the smoker, when they go against the grain and break their destructive habits, initially feel worse than ever. Keep going!

Remember that a Projection is a bad habit, a bad habit of mind. In fighting it, you can expect to experience pain, anxiety, and disorientation just as surely as you would if you went on a strict diet or abruptly stopped smoking.

Remember too that you're fighting *many* habits at one time. A Projection, unlike overeating or smoking, is not composed of only one undesired activity. Nevertheless, you are fighting habits. This means that if you are suffering, you are on the right track. Your outlook is improving, though you can't see this at once. Perhaps at first the only signs of improvement, aside from the pain itself, are certain early suggestions that things look a little different.

In Russ's case, as soon as he starts making some of the changes on the lower rungs of his ladder, hanging on to his marriage will start to seem a little more questionable.

Once he drops his Projection-related habit of speaking deprecatingly about all those who break up marriages and accepts that some may have done what was best for them, *he begins to feel a bit ridiculous in staying unquestioningly with a person he never liked or loved.*

When he ceases treating divorced friends like criminals or pathetic losers and allows himself to see that many are enjoying new and better relationships, and that some are even on good terms with their former mates, who are also flourishing, Russ must change his picture of *himself-after-divorce.* Instead of imagining himself as ostracized and living in some seedy, horrible room, he begins to glimpse the reality that he could be living as comfortably as he is now, as close to his children as ever, but in love with someone who loves him in return.

In the past, by having "lined up" with his Projection of the world as demanding conformity and by "protecting" that Projection, nurturing and supporting it with related activities, Russ kept his distress at a minimum. It was much easier for him to stick it out when he "lined up" behind his choice and reinforced his belief that conformity was necessary. So long as he saw himself-after-divorce as a ruined man, then there was no reasonable conflict. He just resigned himself to doing what it seemed he had to do, stifling the thought of any alternative. On the one occasion when he almost fell in love with another woman, he had downgraded her in his mind, telling himself that she was an enemy to his home.

Now, in the early stages of his suffering, he is allowing

himself to see the possibility of an alternative. In this way he is weakening his Projection: Projections thrive on the ruling out of alternatives.

Always, when you start to break a set pattern of activities—to loosen a Projection—you will at first "hunger" to resume the activity you have stopped. As this hunger increases, you may begin to feel that you cannot survive without satisfying it by returning to your old way. You will start looking for things that you can no longer do, or for terrible dangers that will overtake you without the protection of your projective habit. And the mind is quick to supply these "justifications."

Like someone who's quit smoking and says, "I can't possibly write this report unless I have a cigarette," or an overeater who says, "I'll get sick and die if I don't eat red meat," you will find reasons why these life-support systems of yours are necessary.

But as we have seen, when you let these feelings of "hunger" speak to you, they will lead you to a set of images—maybe nightmare images—that form the picture of your Projection. Remember above all that these are not hungers that you must satisfy. They are part of the system of illusions that you yourself create to justify a return to your old, self-destructive behavior.

You can use this "hunger illusion" to learn more about what you fear, and by naming the fear, deprive it of some of its mystery and power. The "hunger illusion" is also a signal that you are making progress, that you are stopping an activity that has truly been injurious, and that you are securing your perch on this rung of the ladder.

In some cases, the sense of loss in your life that led you to discover your Projection was a dull, persistent pain. You may have been able to forget about it until you lost another job or failed with another lover. In other cases the distress may have been so chronic that you got used to feeling it every day. Heather found going to work a daily nightmare, but it seemed inescapable because *all* bosses were so unfair.

As you go up the ladder, the sort of distress you will feel as you tackle each new change of behavior is a completely different sort of pain. It is far more acute, but it is *temporary.* It is the temporary pain of withdrawal from any habit.

You are totally revamping your behavior. You are jarring your nervous system, which has been slumbering in its old habits, and your distress is caused by the radical novelty of what you are doing. As soon as the novelty wears off, the distress will subside, and your nervous system can go back to normal. New *good* habits of mind will have replaced the old bad ones.

The key to climbing the ladder successfully is knowing what to expect. Your distress will be *acute but brief* at every rung. As you repeat each new behavior, that behavior will become easy—a new good habit replacing an old bad one.

Isn't it better to endure the temporary anxiety of withdrawal and resist your hunger for your old self-destructive habit, than to watch yourself repeat mistakes with people, fear them chronically, fall out of love, and generally get less and less out of life?

7. *Dealing with opposition from others*
As soon as you start "looking different" you can expect some annoying reactions from others. You're doing things that they themselves do normally and that everyone else around them does as a matter of course. But for you, they seem out of character.

For instance, you're fighting the Projection that everyone else is smarter than you. You force yourself to start giving your opinions as others do. To your surprise, a friend says that you're suddenly talking about a lot of things you don't know anything about.

Or you're attacking your Projection that your role to people is that of "doormat to be poked at and kidded." For the first time, you allow yourself to get annoyed when people joke at your expense. A "friend" who's often insulted you comments, "You used to be fun. What's the matter? Why are you suddenly getting so boring and serious?"

Usually you'll be able to predict which people in your life will oppose the new you. Often, they'll be the people closest to you, the people you care most about, the people who've known you the longest.

Obviously, you're not going to back off; not after all the work you've done toward changing. But it's important to remember too that you yourself played into the false impression of you that the other person held, possibly for many, many years.

When opposition comes, you should congratulate yourself. The very fact that people are questioning you shows that you are changing! And the stronger the opposition, the more radical your change must be.

Let's look at a case in point, along with its history.

Jessica says to her sister, Elaine, "I really don't want to meet you that early Saturday morning; I'd like to sleep late."

Elaine replies nastily, "Not before noon? My, my! Aren't you being the big shot!"

Elaine has often made it clear that no one should call *her* before noon on certain weekends. She's proud of her social life and has often taunted Jessica, for instance by mentioning that she was exhausted because she was out dancing very late the night before, or that she went to two parties and they were both terrific.

Now when Jessica is rebuked by her older sister, she remembers these moments and thinks, "So why shouldn't *I* be allowed to sleep late, too?"

Obviously she should have the right, but Elaine doesn't see it that way. She's accustomed to thinking of Jessica as her drab little sister with no social life. Where would Jessica go? Who would take her there?

Since childhood, Jessica's Projection of her sister has been that of "glamorous, sought-after socialite." When Jessica was in elementary school and Elaine was in high school, Jessica often helped her try on fancy dresses for her numerous dates. Jessica would listen wide-eyed as Elaine talked about all the boys who were in love with her and about all the school activity clubs that were begging her to join. Back then, Jessica would even get on the phone for Elaine and tell fibs to boys Elaine was jilting or postponing.

When Elaine went to college, Jessica had pictured her as the campus queen, and Elaine encouraged her to keep thinking of her that way.

Jessica was surprised recently when Elaine got divorced after only a year of marriage. But then it would be hard for someone like Elaine to find a man exciting enough for her.

Then recently Jessica met a man she liked a lot, a fellow student getting his master's degree in education. She immediately established a wonderful rapport with him. She couldn't wait for her sister to meet him.

Jessica was stunned when Elaine was coldly unimpressed. All Elaine could think of to say afterwards was, "I guess he's all right."

What made things worse was that Jessica, in describing her sister to her boyfriend, had portrayed her as terrific. Now Jessica couldn't help feeling that if Elaine were so terrific, she would have taken the trouble to pay a little more attention to the man her sister was in love with.

Meanwhile, Jessica's boyfriend was unimpressed with *Elaine.* He gave Jessica a stiff lecture about building Elaine up too much and running herself down. Jessica had realized he was right. She saw that she hadn't been giving herself her due and yet projected magical glamour and allure onto her sister.

With that insight, Jessica had started pinpointing some of her problem behaviors. She always dressed down. She would never wear a big hat, though she always thought they looked beautiful on other women. She regularly let women friends pick meeting places, as if they somehow would know what was "in" better than she possibly could. When she was with a group of other women, she tended to be quiet. If she was talking to a man and another woman came along and engaged him, she would slip away. There were men she would have liked to date whom she introduced to other women instead. She had thought these men were "too good looking" or "too worldly" for her.

Jessica ordered these behaviors and others she pinpointed in a ladder, from easiest-to-change to hardest-to-change. She had realized right away that changing her behavior with other women would be on the easier rungs. Any revision of her behavior with her sister, however, would be terribly hard, though she didn't know exactly why.

The first change she made was to suggest a restaurant that she'd read about when she and a girlfriend were discussing plans to take a cousin of hers out for her birthday. On the way to the restaurant, Jessica was frightened. "What if they hate the place?" She had a wild image of them calling her crazy and walking away.

She'd had a similar picture when she first bought a low-cut black dress. On the way to a party, she imagined everyone in the room stopping their conversations and laughing at her when she walked in. She forced herself to free associate, using that picture as a starting place. She could hear people saying, "Who does she think she is trying to attract attention like that? She looks ridiculous." Then, she remembered a particular scene from her childhood. She had tried on a dress that her uncle had given her for Christmas and that she loved. Her mother grimaced. "Give that to your sister," she said unhesitatingly. "You have to have a certain flair to wear a dress like that. It overpowers you. You should stick with simple clothes." So she had given the dress to Elaine.

Jessica resisted all those misgivings and also the impulse to turn back and make herself comfortably drab. She walked into the party and nobody laughed. In fact, two women asked her where she'd bought the dress. Obviously, they liked it. She must have looked good in it. Gradually, it became natural for her to choose more glamorous clothing, to arrange evenings for herself and groups of friends, and to speak her mind freely when with other women.

Until that point, all Jessica's struggles had been with herself. No one had opposed the new, outgoing Jessica. In fact, people had enjoyed her more.

Now she was at the top rung of the ladder. She'd known from the beginning that it would be hard to be different with her sister. In fact, in previous weeks, as Elaine's return from her summer in Europe drew closer, Jessica had grown increasingly nervous.

Jessica had been dreading having to tell Elaine that she was going to live with her boyfriend. Her sense was that Elaine would resent this declaration that she had come of age and that she might make a show of objecting on moral grounds, or say that Jessica's boyfriend wasn't good enough for her.

The previous week Jessica and her boyfriend had agreed that Jessica should meet her sister alone the first time after Elaine returned. That was how the insulting phone call came to pass. Jessica had called her older sister in order to meet her and to break the news. After they'd agreed on Saturday, Elaine informed Jessica that she had a busy day and they had better make it at ten in the morning.

Without thinking about it, Jessica replied that it wasn't good for her before noon.

Little had Jessica dreamed that the avalanche would start then and there. She had expected sarcasm when she would tell Elaine the big news about living with her boyfriend. But Elaine had picked up on her very first sentence! She didn't even let Jessica get started.

Even before the anticipated showdown, she violently opposed the new Jessica—the one without the subservient Projection. But Jessica stuck to her position and held fast.

This kind of opposition tells you two things. First, it tells you loud and clear that if you aren't to be run over and go right back to square one, you must follow through with what you've started. Second, it delivers the wonderful news that you are already a new person. The disproportionate violence of Jessica's sister's reaction to a simple request indicated that her universe had been shattered. It seems Elaine realized immediately that she was talking to a different person. She was aware that Jessica had climbed to her level, that Jessica no longer saw *her* as the princess, and that from now on, Jessica would expect equal treatment.

On your way up the ladder, never let the dismay of others goad you into turning back to resume your old style of behavior.

You may have an impulse to conclude, "If my husband is going to be this upset with me, why should I keep talking about getting a job?" or, "If my daughter is going to be ashamed of me, maybe I shouldn't remarry." But remember that this kind of thinking has done you a great disservice, and it will continue to if you let it.

Sometimes, opposition takes the form of advice.

"It's not good for you to be so outspoken in the office."

"It's dangerous to give up your job to do freelance work."

"You shouldn't trust *any* man, particularly one you're in love with!"

Such advice can make it seem even *more* tempting to fall in with the opposition and go back to your old, comfortable identity. But again, *don't!*

Instead, realize that you're being paid an implicit compliment. And aghast opposition means you've really changed.

It hardly needs saying that the ultimate opponents of any basic change in your makeup are your parents. Not that they're necessarily against you, but they've seen you one way—dependent, needing them, uncertain—for a long time. They've become accustomed to seeing themselves as having a certain role in your life. Your maturity may be a crisis for them.

In any event, nearly all opposition comes from people who have their own Projections on you. Those who oppose you imagine that they have something to lose if you change. But in reality, they have much to gain from your development.

True, Jessica's sister lost a worshipper when Jessica reached her level. But she gained a friend.

The key to dealing with opposition is to approach it confidently. Assume that opposition, like the other forms of discomfort you are experiencing, is temporary. As you continue, people will get used to you; if they don't, it will cease to matter to you nearly as much as it does now.

8. *Succeeding*

You've ascended the rungs of the ladder and made yourself secure on each one by repeating the new behavior with which you replaced your old self-defeating Projection. In turn, each new behavior has become effortless and natural. Together, all the new behaviors that you've mastered create and sustain a new and better outlook, one that allows you to see others more realistically. The temporary anxiety of withdrawal from your old habits of mind is gone, and you may find it hard even to remember the way you used to see people.

You no longer feel that you're doing anything to deliberately construct an outlook. In fact, without even being aware of it, you will go on bringing other behaviors "into line" with your new outlook. The law of consonance will prompt you to add actions unconsciously that are consistent with your new way of looking at people. You feel comfortable acting in accordance with your perceptions. The only difference is that now, you'll feel good about what you're doing *and* about the results.

For example, as Joel made a habit of revealing his uncertainty, asking for help, admitting his mistakes, and not boasting, it became natural for him to see that people genuinely liked him for who he was. He saw that he had no need for grandiose pretense. He overcame his feeling that everyone would laugh at him or disown him if he blundered. He actually developed much closer relationships once he was no longer obsessed with the possibility of failure.

In the other case, as Heather taught herself to see her boss as an individual, she began to genuinely enjoy her job. She dropped all the time-consuming extra gimmicks for ingratiating herself with Anne and instead applied all her energy to her work. She was delighted when Anne responded by publicly praising her and then promoting her. Gradually, it became impossible for Heather to even imagine that Anne would bring anything other than performance criteria to her judgement of an employee. As she taught herself to see that her career was in her own hands, Heather also felt freer about speaking to Anne as a person. She realized that Anne was not a wicked stepmother figure but a young woman close to her own age, and a good friend. The very behavior that had brought about Heather's new perception, mastered at the cost of considerable anxiety along the way, now seemed like a natural expression of her feelings toward Anne. When Heather herself later became a supervisor, she had strong ideas about what kind of boss *she* wanted to be, and a keen perception of which of her colleagues were good or bad managers.

All psychotherapy, to the degree that it helps the patient develop new perceptions of others, does so in just the way we've described. The patient identifies his perception—his Projection—and pinpoints many behaviors that go with it. Usually the therapist belongs to some "school" and has some kind of theory that explains why the patient sees others as he does. "Heather, you hate bosses because of an Oedipus Complex, according to which you're competitive with your mother." Or, "Heather, you have an Adlerian inferiority complex and therefore hate all female authority figures." The therapist helps the patient see a dozen ways that the patient *acts* which exemplify the problem. While patient and therapist talk about the patient's childhood and early life (the so-called cause of the problem), the patient, without necessarily being told to do so, goes out and *acts* differently. *Whatever the theory, the real leverage for change of outlook is what the patient does.* The new behavior causes anxiety at first but gradually changes the person's perception.

Meanwhile, analyst and patient may go on talking about what they see as the "root" of the problem—Oedipal or inferiority complex or birth trauma or whatever. It's a huge irony that when the patient develops a new perception and solves the problem—and is therefore cured—both patient and analyst may attribute the cure to their deep understanding of the imaginary root. The Oedipal theorist imagines that he has proven the relevance of the Oedipus Complex one more time. The Adlerian imagines he has proven Adler's greatness, and so on. But in each case, the patient has himself produced the cure in exactly the manner described in this chapter.

All therapy, if it succeeds, works by the patient's producing the cure through identifying the problem outlook, pinpointing the attendant behavior, and changing that behavior, changing the outlook.

SUMMARY

You can change your own outlook because of a simple truth: Projections require constant sustenance. If you don't act on them, they'll die.

After identifying the Projection you want to change, it becomes important to pinpoint as many of the behaviors connected with it as you can. When you set out to break a Projection, you are really breaking an interconnected set of bad habits.

Order those bad habits—projective behaviors—in a ladder from "easiest-to-change" to "hardest-to-change." Realize that in some cases, you'll be eliminating behaviors entirely and in others you'll be replacing them with new behaviors.

You can expect plenty of anxiety along the way. To change is always harder than to stay the same, and even change for the better often feels strange and somehow wrong. But remember, the anxiety that you're feeling now is simply the pain of withdrawal. It is temporary, and as you repeat your new behaviors, it will subside and eventually disappear altogether.

When you finally reach the top of the ladder, having secured yourself on each successive rung, you will *be* a new person. Your outlook will be free, confident, and healthy. You will see love and friendship as available, and indeed, they will be available. You will sense accurately whom to choose and whom to avoid.

Unfortunately, your new outlook doesn't come with a lifetime guarantee. But you can provide that guarantee yourself by knowing a few more facts.

8

HOW CAN YOU
STAY CLEAR-MINDED
ABOUT PEOPLE?

Suppose two people confined in separate prison cells for a long period are each given a deck of cards and allowed to play solitaire. One plays as well as he can within the rules, keeping a careful record of how well he does at the game. He works at improving his skills. The other gets disgusted with his results and begins to cheat.

The honest player has given himself something to look forward to. Right after breakfast, he's eager to get started playing. Each day he sets out to beat his record of games won, and today he won a game he would have lost last week. He anticipates further improvement.

The cheat has killed the game for himself. It holds no challenge, no interest; it's nothing to look forward to. Now he's trying to think of other ways to pass a few hours, but nothing comes to mind. He's bored and depressed, and his life is empty compared with the honest player's.

The honest player has projected value and optimism on the trivial game of solitaire. He pays his dues by following the rules, and the game gives him a lot back. The dishonest player has destroyed the game's usefulness in his life. He has taken a potentially meaningful and joyous activity away from himself. His projection is that solitaire, like the rest of his life, is a waste of time.

We've all met the man who whines that he just keeps falling out of love. In the beginning he drives us crazy rhapsodizing about the woman he's just met. But a few months later, he's desperate to get rid of her.

And we all know someone who changes jobs every year, always starting out with high hopes and then leaving disillusioned. He tells us that the boss was not the "mover" he seemed to be, and therefore, the operation fell far short of its promise.

We see the same thing in friendship. There are some who always seem excited about the newest people on their horizon but who can't name one individual they've been close to for as long as five years.

The problem with all these people is that they fail to *act* in ways that project value, importance, or desirability.

The man who falls out of love, assuming that he hasn't really made impossible choices each time, has omitted an ingredient necessary if a love affair is to last. He has failed to act in ways that would keep him in love. He might say, "What do *I* care if I stay in love? Those women turned out to be boring pains in the neck." But his first impressions weren't always so wrong. At least some of the women *were* alluring and vital, precisely what he wanted in a woman and thought he had found. It wasn't the *woman* who changed but *his view of her*. By his failure to act in ways that would project "beloved" onto a woman, he gradually taught himself to project "insufficient" onto to them. By persuading himself that the women were unlovable, he thus robbed himself of love.

The analogy applies to staying "in love with" a boss or a friend or an idea, or humankind itself.

If you can't, you may deprive yourself of anything and everything you ever wanted. You're in the same position as the person who is left by a lover or who truly can't find one; you're as badly off as someone who is fired repeatedly for incompetence or who can't make friends because of social ineptitude. The only difference is that *you made yourself a loser.* Everything you wanted was there for you, you *had* it, but you gradually poisoned it. *You couldn't continue seeing your happiness, so you stopped being happy.*

This is a subtle concept. It is very different from saying that you should just look "on the bright side," or that you should be happy with less. We're talking about the need to preserve what really *is* precious to you.

AXIOM XXIX: You are the only one who can make a relationship desirable to yourself.

AXIOM XXX: By the same token, it is within *your* power to poison your happiness by stripping the desirability from your relationships. By your actions, you can persuade yourself that your relationships really aren't so precious.

BUILDING
RELATIONSHIPS TO LAST

Many of us complain that our relationships don't last, but then, we haven't constructed them to last. We choose a car that will last just a few good years, and some of us do the same when choosing friends and lovers. Those with this problem would rarely consider studying how to build broad-based friendships or how to make either love or sex endure. Rather, the emphasis is on getting what they want as soon as they can and keeping it till it doesn't work any more.

It's not just that such people use the wrong criteria when selecting partners for friendships, marriages, and other relationships. Even if they have selected the "right" partner, those who view everything as dispensable often *treat* their partners in ways that *make the them seem less desirable* than they originally did.

The mate or friend we once cherished may not have changed, but because of the way *we* have treated him, he or she appears to have changed. He now looks boring or stingy or dishonest. It is crucial to our happiness that we learn to preserve our sense of other people's desirability through our actions toward them.

Many who claim to be unlucky in love and friendship would also say that to know people is to discover how disappointing they really are. Friendship is brittle; love and sexuality are inevitably brief. Such people can often cite a list of those they once adored, including perhaps a former mate or two, who revealed a new, negative side to their personalities almost at once. They can list friends who seemed exciting at first but turned out to be duds, and jobs they took that looked great in the offing but that went stale within months.

At the other extreme are people who by habit build relationships to last. They may begin cautiously, but their natural style encourages friendships to grow and to endure. They take pains to survive the difficult periods that beset any longstanding friendship or marriage and emerge from those periods closer to the other person than ever. When they are old, they can nearly always boast of troops of friends; they have around them people at many different levels of nearness—from nodding acquaintances to confidants and soul mates.

The very clarity of vision that enables them to sustain the benefits of friendships keeps them out of the orbit of those who would weaken them or hurt them. They shun hangers-on and ill-wishers. These clear-eyed people with the courage of their opinions have no stake in holding onto bad relationships just out of fear of being alone. The same sighting system that makes them sensitive to all the *good* things their friends do alerts them to bad intentions in others. They recognize those who are toxic to them. They don't pretend that all is well when it isn't, nor do they censor themselves when they spot trouble. They automatically lower their esteem for anyone who has abused them or who violates their ethical standards. They can sever relationships altogether when an offense warrants it.

The ability of these people to discern good from bad is an enhancement to their real friends, who always feel appreciated and understood. They give credit for longevity in relationships, extending a kind of seniority to those who have proven their loyalty. These people, who build relationships to last, typically feel that at no other time in history and in no other place has such a coterie of loving and loyal friends as theirs existed.

Both the people who enjoy relationships for a lifetime and those who build a self-destruct mechanism into every new relationship imagine that they are merely seeing people as they are, and treating them accordingly. Ordinarily, they overlook the role that their own actions have played, one way or the other. For the former, that role was to *enhance* other people in their own minds. For the latter, it was to *downgrade* people in their minds, to project onto others traits that made them seem like disappointments. Without their knowing it, the former have made themselves feel lucky, and the latter have made themselves feel unlucky by sabotaging what was given to them.

AXIOM XXXI: Success in any relationship requires that you go on *enhancing* the other person in your own mind. If you *downgrade* someone, you will teach yourself that your relationship with that person is neither desirable nor precious.

When you routinely turn people into "disappointments," you have very little chance of forming and sustaining any relationship that will keep you happy. And because no one likes to be around a disappointed person, you also pay the price of being undesirable yourself.

AXIOM XXXII: If you are not to ruin people for yourself and destroy your vision of those who could provide your primary chances for happiness, you must avoid any actions that whittle other people down in your esteem and make them look like disappointments to you.

There are a number of behaviors that may be dangerous to your view of others, ways in which you may act that will make people look unworthy to you.

You may, for instance, get caught up in doing too much for a lover or friend and come to resent him, or you may demand so much that you come to see the person as existing only for your convenience. By lying to a person or tricking him repeatedly, you may come to see him as stupid. By insulting a person or by being repeatedly uncaring toward him, you may teach yourself to despise him, and so forth.

The other person, assuming he is unskilled in defending his image, is almost sure to fall prey to your downgrading behavior.

Through no fault of his own, he will lose status in your eyes. And, of course, you will be the loser too, whether or not you may blame him for letting you down. If you had enhanced him in your own mind, rather than downgrading him, you might have been able to delight in that person's virtues for a lifetime. Tonight, you'd be telling people you were lucky to know him.

Deriving less from people is never a mark of personal excellence.

It's not enough merely to *have* a desirable relationship. You must *protect* the desirability of what you have. Just as you would set up a security system to protect your home and loved ones, you must take precautions to protect your ability to *enjoy* the people you treasured at the outset.

THE LAW
OF ECONOMY
——

The most usual process by which we downgrade people unknowingly we may think of as succumbing to the Law of Economy.

Built into each of us is a desire to simplify, to streamline our behavior. As we learn anything, we tend to retain the minimum amount of activity necessary to get a thing done and drop extra behaviors as soon as we realize they aren't essential.

For instance, when you first learned to cook, you probably apportioned all your ingredients precisely, using various measuring implements. You may have laid out those ingredients in advance. You checked your cookbook repeatedly, not trusting yourself. After a time, you gradually smoothed out your performance, dropping features that seemed useless. Now, you can make your favorite dishes on the run, measuring by eye. If someone were to ask you for a recipe, you would actually have to think about what you did, because your preparations have become so automatic.

Learning anything involves this smoothing-out process, this economy.

Even more smoothing out occurs as you perfect the activity. Concurrently with the simplification of the process, you lose awareness that you are doing the thing at all. You simply do the thing, whether it's walking or cooking or typing a letter or driving a car. In childhood, when you first learned a simple activity such as combing your hair, it took deliberation and attention; now you do it automatically, while contemplating the day's activities or talking to another person.

This introduction of economy, in both physical action and thought, occurs no matter what we are learning. We go from doing the thing awkwardly with extra motions and a certain amount of concentration to doing it more simply and with little or no thought. This simplification, once necessary for survival in the wild, is just as necessary for us today. Unless we learned to smooth out our behavior this way, we might spend our whole day caught up in a handful of acts no more complex than tying a shoelace.

In dealing with people as well, there's a tendency toward such "economy." But here, such a reduction of effort can be dangerous.

Larry, a good-looking man of thirty-three, was one of those people who was always falling out of love, who was always disappointed. He would complain that after an exuberant start, the decline would begin almost immediately. He would try to push away his initial doubts, but before he knew it, he was lying awake in bed cursing himself for having promised too much to the wrong woman. Finally, he would walk out.

Larry construed himself wholly as a victim of women who let him down. He saw himself as sincerely searching for the right woman the way Parsifal sought the Holy Grail. When he first met Olivia, he was sure that she was the woman of his dreams. She was a book reviewer for a good newspaper, and Larry glowed whenever she complimented him on a turn of phrase. Every day he looked for her byline and if he saw it, was overjoyed. He avidly read every line, calling her afterwards to say how wonderful a piece was or meeting her for lunch to tell her.

In those early days, Larry studied Olivia's wants, delighted in her friends, and tried to think of things to do for her that no one else would think of.

As a college writing teacher, Larry didn't have much weekday time to himself. He normally reserved weekends for his own writing, which was precious to him. Still, he took many weekends off from the long novel he was trying to complete to spend time with Olivia. He would invite her to hear his college lectures, and he enjoyed reading poetry to her. Finally, he told her he loved her.

She said she wasn't sure about him; it seemed she was still getting over a man in her recent past. But, after three months, Olivia made up her mind. She said she loved Larry too.

It was at about this time that Larry felt the need to go back to his novel. He explained to her that he'd been shirking his responsibility to himself, and she understood.

At first, he'd give her several hours notice if he was immersed in his work and wanted to cancel dinner: "I'll be over around ten. I really can't leave just now." Soon, he began making the same kind of phone call if a few friends dropped over to watch a football game on TV. He'd ask them to turn down the set so that Olivia would assume that he was writing. It seemed more economical than having to explain what was really going on.

By the sixth month, he often omitted the phone call that would have freed her to do something else while he was busy. He also stopped reading her reviews: His own book was going badly, and it was painful to read about other writers who were doing well.

By then, Larry was no longer looking for things to *do* for Olivia. In fact, he was looking for things *not* to do. He started asking *her* to run errands for *him,* "since you're downtown anyway." He had streamlined his dealings with her, reducing them to only those activities necessary to placate her, to keep her from ditching him.

It *wasn't* simply that Larry was falling out of love and therefore doing less for Olivia. His every "economy" was altering his Projection of Olivia as the woman of his dreams. By treating her steadily worse, he was teaching himself to see her as a utility, not the woman he would spend his life with. And she played into her new identity by settling for less and going along with him.

Initially, his disappointment was only slight. His doubts about her came and went, like the shadow of a bird. After all, he still enjoyed sex with her, though he made it more brief, and he liked having her there on certain weekends. Besides, he often found it easier to write when she was in the other room and when he knew that she would be available the moment he left the typewriter.

Then one day Larry received a harsh rejection letter from a magazine editor in response to an article he'd submitted.

He felt miserable. When he asked Olivia for her opinion, she disagreed with the editor and told Larry she believed in his talent. Unexpectedly, he whirled on her in anger, defending the critic's position and accusing her of trying merely to pacify him.

"Praise when I do a bad job is the last thing I need," he said, and she cried.

Soon he was picturing himself with another woman—and giving almost nothing to Olivia. The less he gave, the less he loved her, or even liked her. He insisted that they take a three-month break, not seeing each other or even talking during that time so that they could think things over. She protested vehemently, which only served to lower his respect for her even more.

A month later he got a message that she'd called, but he didn't call her back.

Then Larry got a phone call from Olivia telling him that she'd fallen in love with another man, a young, best-selling novelist she'd interviewed. "He's asked me to marry him, and I'm going to."

Larry could hardly believe it. Had he made a mistake? He remembered those early magical days with Olivia when he'd read Proust to her in a rowboat on the lake and they'd talked about living together. He tried to console himself by returning to his novel, pursuing his love affair with posterity now that Olivia was gone. But it was terribly lonely. He realized that he might have better striven for posterity with her at his side.

Larry had fallen out of love, exactly as he had many times before. It wasn't that he'd lost Olivia by not measuring up. Nor was it simply that he'd antagonized her. The problem was that he'd stopped doing those things necessary for *him* to stay in love. He'd destroyed her desirability to him. He'd imagined that he could get away with doing only what was convenient. But by "economizing" in his treatment of her, he ruined his glorious image of her and the special quality of their relationship. As Jean-Paul Sartre said, "There is no such thing as love but only acts of loving."

It's important to realize that Larry *was* in love with Olivia at the time she said she loved him. He'd been wonderfully happy, as he told his friends. Larry's fatal step was to cut back on effort, attentiveness, and involvement with Olivia's life, because he thought that he could do so without loss— that he *had* her. This decline, this worse treatment, led Larry to start *seeing* Olivia in a new, unfavorable way. By his *actions,* Larry convinced himself that Olivia was not "beloved."

Once they were apart and Larry was no longer able to mistreat Olivia, to "economize" at her expense, the images of her glory returned. During the weeks and months after he received Olivia's last phone call, he saw the other guy as "lucky," and Olivia as "terrific." Larry believed he'd never meet anyone like her again.

People like Larry, whose relationships follow this pattern of economy followed by disillusionment, are familiar to most of us. We marvel at how such an attractive, intelligent, and successful man or woman who apparently wants a relationship can fail so often. We can't figure out why.

Often there's an interesting giveaway that the Law of Economy is at work. The person may be really in love with someone who is unattainable for any of a number of reasons—for instance, his dream partner has gone away, died, been lost to the past, or is married to someone else. Larry told Olivia on one of their first dates that he'd always had a crush on the wife of a colleague. However, Larry added, the woman was crazy about her husband, who was no genius in Larry's estimation. For years, Larry had had to settle for seeing her at faculty parties once a semester.

Others like Larry find that they can only fall in love if the other person is very much younger or older and would never take them seriously. They can only go on treasuring a person when they've had no chance to devalue that person by the way they deal with her. It's not that familiarity breeds contempt, but that familiarity gives these people the opportunity to create contempt.

Nearly any "liberty" that we take, if the underlying reason for it is even a slight decline of respect for a person, contributes to further loss of respect. It might be as flagrant as an extramarital affair or subtler, such as making a snide comment about the person to a third party. Or it could even be our discussion of some subject that the person wouldn't want us to talk about. We snap an order, we stop putting up the morning coffee the way we used to, we ask the other person to turn out the light we left on, we indulge in nagging or making requests.

No single act means much, but an accumulation of acts like these, acts that we would not have dared at the outset of a relationship, makes the person seem more mundane, less worthy of sacrifice, no longer a privilege to know.

If we followed it literally the Law of Economy would have us smooth out all our behavior with people, doing less and less for them, until ultimately we performed only acts we felt were absolutely necessary for our purposes.

We might start out buying presents for a lover, saying please and thank you, calling up to see how he or she did in the big meeting, proceeding elaborately when we made love, only to "simplify" that behavior as we went along. Gradually we would dispense with the presents and amenities; our lovemaking would diminish in subtlety and intensity, becoming quick and to the point. Succumbing to the Law of Economy, we would rob the relationship of what made it special, of its richness. We would make it as cut and dried as other habitual activities, like driving a car.

That is, we would make this mistake *unless* we realized that all our acts—including the supporting ones as well as the truly essential ones—have values of their own and cannot be dispensed with. The real consequences of acts—saying please or thank you, choosing our outfits with care, calling to see how a person is doing, making love, going to a wedding or funeral—include their effects on *our picture of other people* and *on our relationships.*

Not realizing the real importance of small acts, millions fall victim to the Law of Economy in relationships. By cutting back on their efforts when things seem good enough, they destroy the special feeling they had about the other person. Theirs is an economy far more costly than they realize.

Often the decline in our efforts, which both causes and is produced by a loss of respect for the other person, starts in response to a specific signal.

For Larry, Olivia's saying, "I love you," was the signal. And there are men who suddenly treat women differently when the woman becomes pregnant or has children. These men may replace the laughter and freedom of romance with a new reverence and thereby unwittingly kill their sexual desire and romantic feelings for their wives.

Or the signal for change may be a rumor we hear about another person. We find out that someone we knew and trusted has a prison record. That was long ago, and he's been honorable with us, but we begin to treat him differently. Soon we are seeing him not as the person he has been with us but as an ex-con. Any discovery of a fact about a person may become a signal for us to stereotype him. If we don't want to change his meaning in our life and lose the benefit of his friendship, we had better not downgrade our treatment of him in reaction to what we have just learned about him.

AXIOM XXXIII: Whether in response to a specific signal, such as suddenly knowing for sure that a person is committed to you, or as a general time-reflex in relationships, cutting back to worse treatment is always a false economy with a friend or lover.

AXIOM XXXIV: By withholding or by conserving effort for other activities at the expense of a friend or loved one, you are propagandizing yourself against that person. You run the risk of "ruining" that person for yourself, of losing the happiness you could share with him.

MIMICKING

A second common practice whose unseen effect is to cause Projections destructive to us is to mimic behavior we don't really believe in, simply because "everyone does it."

For the sake of your own clear view of people, it's important that you act in accordance with a standard that you yourself set and never lapse into treating people or institutions in ways that will lower your esteem for them merely because others act that way.

Remember that in the end, you must live with whatever Projections you create and sustain. No matter what others do, or exhort you to do, you are the one who will have to take the consequences of losing relationships and losing your bearing and sense of direction in life, if you act in ways that destroy your joy of life. You may come to see the world as a chaotic place where only those who devote themselves to beating the system can survive.

Others may engage in behavior that is in vogue but that would be abhorrent in an ideal world. A lover may use devices in dealing with you that downgrade you: tricks such as trying to make you jealous or getting you to give more than you want to by making you feel guilty. Oppose those devices, but don't mimic them. To mimic any such device is to excuse it in your own mind and possibly to become dependent upon it yourself.

You may feel especially tempted to mimic behavior in the office. There you may feel it's excusable to act in ways that you would never consider in your personal life.

For instance, Evelyn has a job she basically likes and a boss who is fair to her. But she sees other employees taking office supplies, going home early, pretending they're ill when they're not. She is one of a few who play by the book. And it's often hard.

The office cynics tell her that she's got to be a fool to work as hard as she does. Her inclination is not to listen to them, but it hurts when, in spite of her sincere efforts, the boss awards a special, high-commission account to a phoney whose manipulations took him in.

Evelyn considers going in to the boss and presenting her case, but she doesn't. Instead, she goes out for drinks with a few disgruntled co-workers, who advise her to get even with the boss by padding her expense account. One of them reminds her, "Everybody does it."

While Evelyn is thinking it over, a few others chime in. "You'd be crazy not to."

"Don't you think *he'd* do it if he was in your position? How do you think he got where he is?"

Evelyn has always felt that this particular little group was a bit below par, especially the guy who's been egging her on. She doesn't much like his attitude at work or, for that matter, the way he talks to his wife when she picks him up. But as what they're saying starts to sink in, it doesn't seem so wrong. A bigger company *would* pay her much more for the same job. A lot of bosses wouldn't have been taken in like that and would have given *Evelyn* the account with all that money attached to it. So maybe there would even be a curious fairness to making it up on her expense account.

Once again the ringleader prods her, "Why not?"

This sharpens the dilemma. The arguments for taking the extra money are so obvious a child could grasp them. Evelyn could replace her stereo system and buy her daughter a better wardrobe for her month in camp.

On the other hand, the case against it is subtle, having to do with the *effects that Evelyn could expect to occur in her own outlook.*

Already she senses that there will be some fallout regarding how she sees herself, the boss, and people in general. She has a vague apprehension that she's entering another kind of life. Feeling suddenly exhausted, she decides to go home.

With a knowledge of Projection, Evelyn would be able to see more precisely why she was so drained by anticipation of this new behavior. Were she to embark on the new lifestyle and persist in it, were she to do dishonest things repeatedly, she would ultimately make it seem to herself *that she had no alternative.* Her view of people and the world would undergo a marked change. No longer would she picture her co-workers as dishonest; it would seem that they were only doing what was necessary. And her projection on the few honest people left in the office would also change. She would soon start to see them as foolish or as just too timid to take care of themselves the way smart people do. The boss himself would loom as an adversary, and with her previously high opinion of him destroyed by her new behavior toward him—cheating him—she would find it much harder to face him directly and ask for what she wanted.

There would be broader effects too, changes in her vision

of humankind in general and of the world as an environment. Were Evelyn herself to break the faith, the world would come to seem a dangerous place, where eternal vigilance is necessary.

When you violate any ethic, you inevitably alter your sense of what *ought* to be. By mimicking the dishonesty that once felt wrong to you and that you would have deplored, by repeating such behavior and by making a habit of it, you make dishonesty look necessary, and you make your life much harder than it has to be. Incredulous of human goodness, you condemn yourself to a hook-or-crook life, where there seems constant need to protect yourself and to plan ahead. You feel that nothing good can ever come to you unless you seize it by your own cunning.

Mimicking even one act that doesn't sit right with you will foster such a Projection a little bit.

AXIOM XXXV: Acting in ways that you once deplored using the excuse that "everyone does it," will alter your outlook and muddy your view of people and the world. The problem is not that such behavior will always feel *wrong* to you, but rather that soon it will feel *right* and necessary.

A common form of mimicking, nearly always self-destructive, is *retaliation*—getting even by doing something that you considered wrong when another person did it to you. Revenge always brings satisfaction for the moment, but it also creates a Projection that is harmful to you because it somewhat *excuses* the injury the person has done to you.

A lover has an affair with one of your friends. You get even by having an affair with one of hers. Your best friend excludes you from a holiday weekend at his country house. You retaliate by leaving him off your guest list for Christmas dinner when you know he'll be alone.

It's an illusion that you're *merely* getting even. Admittedly, you're hurt by what the other person did to you. But by your action you're telling yourself that what he did was acceptable: it must be, because you're doing the same thing. This is especially harmful. So long as you can see his action as unacceptable, as unwarranted, as vicious, you can feel separate from that person and go on with your life. He remains to you "one of a kind" instead of an example of "the way of the world."

In a curious sense, though you don't mean to, you're actually forgiving the person when you retaliate in kind. You're making the other person more important in your mind every time you take revenge—and in general, you're overemphasizing the importance of other people's opinions.

Malcolm X, who gave his life trying to right injustices to blacks, begged black employees not to steal when they worked for whites. He pointed out that for centuries blacks in subjection often retaliated by petty theft, on the grounds that what they did was small retribution for the brutality that whites had shown them. But, he argued, blacks must not weaken their own sense of dignity, their vision of what they deserve. By "retaliating" in this small way, he said, blacks were weakening their sense of outrage and entitlement and in effect postponing the day when they would feel strong enough as a group to oppose the real injustices against them. Malcolm X was talking straight Projection theory.

In order to preserve our own sense of dignity and our vision of what we deserve and what ought to be, we must avoid using techniques we deplore. We must not succumb to using any tactic merely because others use it or because we want to retailate.

YOUR PROJECTION
ON LIFE IN GENERAL
———

As long as you live, it will remain within your power to sustain your happiness. You can make the world seem desirable or dismal by choosing either to enhance or downgrade it.

In reality, the world still contains the same fraction of creative people, of generous people, of heroes and lovers and loyal friends, of prospects as it always did. But if you have allowed yourself to snatch short-term gains and to downgrade people—especially those you deal with daily— you will lose your recognition of the magic in people and your ability to be moved by them.

If you choose the easy route of guardedness, pessimism, and doubt, if you stop taking chances, people will move away from you. Rather than offer you friendship and opportunity, they'll avoid the disillusionment they associate with you. Who wants you in a job or a love affair if you don't believe in achievement or love? They'd rather take their chances with a lesser intellect or a less attractive person who brightens their day and participates in life's gambles. You've arranged it so that nothing bad happens, but nothing good happens either. It will be hard for you to truly say, "I have lived."

If you default, you may remember the bright optimism you had when you were young—your former ability to see beauty and not to be dismayed by dishonesty or greed. But now that view appears to you as the naïveté of youth. It will seem to you that your present outlook is accurate and that your earlier one was a distortion.

In fact, it's the other way around. Over the years, you forfeited the exuberant view, the optimistic one, for a picture of people and life that offers little or no pleasure. You unknowingly *did away with* your former view, surrendering it little by little through the behavior you chose.

It's not even a matter of which view is the realistic one. For every pessimist, for every person who sees the world as a "theatre of sin and suffering" (as the German philosopher Authur Schopenhauer put it), there are others who see it as the golden age in progress. Walt Whitman, who knew the Civil War and went to his share of premature funerals, reminds us,

> There was never any more creation than there is now,
> Or any more living or dying than there is now.
> Urge, and urge, and urge.
> Always the procreant urge of the world.

If you have the courage to keep an open, and what some would call "naive" outlook, then people will consider you eternally youthful and be attracted to you. When you trust people, take risks, and allow yourself to be exuberant, people will gravitate toward you and welcome you as a positive force. You'll lose the respect of only the cynic and the arch pessimist, and usually they are people whose own lives are failures anyhow.

SUMMARY

Your happiness and your enjoyment of life are very much within your power.

When you routinely turn people into disappointments, you have very little chance of forming and sustaining any relationship that will keep you happy. How you treat the people you care about will determine whether you *keep* caring about them.

Resist the impulse to cut back on your efforts with people once you feel they are committed to you. The natural human tendency to "economize" in all endeavors amounts to a real danger if you give into it and "streamline" your relationships too much.

Nearly any liberty that you take with someone close to you can erode your sense of that person's desirability. And a pattern of such liberties can destroy a relationship.

Also, resist invitations to act in a certain way because "others do it all the time." If you give in to mimicking behavior that feels wrong to you, you will alter your picture of people and the world. The problem is not that such behavior will *always* feel wrong to you, but rather that soon it will feel right and necessary to you.

If you enhance people in your own mind by the ways you treat them, you will continue to draw pleasure from them and remain happy with them. If you downgrade people by treating them badly, you will "ruin" them for yourself, and you will blind yourself to the possibility of happiness, which may be right at hand.

9

LIVING, LOVING, AND LYING

Now that you understand the Projection Principle, you're ready to see a wide range of everyday behaviors in a totally new light. The Projection Principle illuminates what people are *really* doing to themselves and to others when they use certain very common devices.

Volumes have been written about why particular strategies we use with other people are good or bad—in business, in friendship, in love. Nearly always the aim of these strategies is to get people to respond well to us. Ways of treating people that do this are considered successful, and those that alienate people are not.

But you may have long suspected that this oversimplifies

the issue. Instinct has probably told you that most tactics designed to guarantee a response, though they may work in the short run, will cost you in the end. Even if the other person responds to you as you wish at the moment, you have, by the very act of using a strategy, added an unsavory element to your relationship. As time goes by, you will pay a subtle price for your use of the tactic and, in the long run, your relationship will suffer.

On the other hand, you may have felt that a direct, open approach that takes its chances on the other person's response is the one more likely to make you happy.

Now that you understand that a person's actions produce and sustain Projections, it will be easy for you to see why. As people relate to each other, a great deal more is going on beneath the surface than they realize. Every time someone uses a tactic, there's a *visible* effect, namely, whether it seems to work or not. But there's also a *hidden* effect: the tactic's influence on the user's own outlook. Sometimes even when a strategy of ours succeeds with another person, it has damaging effects on the relationship that more than offset its benefits.

If, while winning someone's favor (say, getting the person to fall in love with you), you are simultaneously teaching yourself to feel contempt for the person, you have lost. Okay, the person now loves you, but as we have seen, if *you've* fallen out of love with him, you have failed as badly as if the person had walked out on you.

Similarly, there are many tactics people use to achieve their ends that sensitive people feel are wrong. Until now those of us who decry such methods have felt that we could do so only on moral grounds. But the Projection Principle gives you a sound psychological basis to demonstrate that what you have felt all your life is true.

When you apply the Projection Principle to activities to

see what their real impact is, you'll find in many cases that it is quite different from what it appears to be.

In this chapter we want to examine some fundamental kinds of behavior from the point of view of what their Projections are. In particular, let's look at manipulation, pretense, giving as a tactic, and several common forms of dishonesty.

MANIPULATION

Mental health professionals talk a lot about *manipulation*— one person treating another in some special way calculated to control his behavior. Here are three examples:

"Hello, Dan. It's Lisa. My phone was ringing when I walked into the apartment and I couldn't get to it. I thought it might be you since you used to call evenings around this time."

In this case, Lisa was concealing her real motive for calling Dan, which was to connect with him and set up a date. Dan had implied that Lisa shouldn't call *him* next time, that he'd call *her* when he was ready. She was afraid that if she told him why she was really calling, he'd ditch her outright.

"Gee, Peggy, I'm glad you're going to Mexico with your boyfriend for two weeks. I saw the doctor today and he said I probably wouldn't have a heart attack right away. I guess he'll have to make up his mind about surgery pretty soon."

Peggy's mother once had a slight heart murmur, now under control. Mainly, she's feeling lonely and she doesn't like Peggy favoring a man's company over hers.

"If you really felt a part of this organization, Jodie, you wouldn't ask for overtime pay to help out in an emergency.

And just because it's on a weekend! I'm working too, you know."

A clever boss can squeeze two advantages out of a comment like this. By instilling guilt, he can get an employee to do extra work for nothing. And the same guilt will deter the employee from asking for a well-deserved raise. After all, she was all ready to let down her organizational "family."

What defines manipulation is that your real motive is hidden so that the other person will do what you want *without knowing what it is that you want.*

Though no one likes the idea of manipulation, few of us can forego it entirely. It's at the core of advertising, and we've come to expect it of politicians and maybe of lawyers. You'd like your product advertised so that it can compete with rival products for the same market; you want your lawyer to use his wiles to counterbalance those of an adversary.

But the more personal the relationship, the more you really care about the other person, the worse manipulation begins to seem. Nearly everybody has a sense that it's wrong to manipulate a loved one or to use the tactic around sex, as in the classic promise "I'll help you with your career if you'll go to bed with me."

And it's no fun to *be* manipulated. When you recognize that someone has used the tactic on you, you may feel cheated out of your freedom or underestimated. Most of us try to discourage manipulativeness, feeling somehow that it's wrong to do. But psychology, which rarely studies how acts affect the actor, has told us little about how the tactic harms the manipulator himself.

The Projection Principle focuses sharply on how manipulation actually hurts the manipulator. Underlying all manipulation of another person is the idea that if you use the right trick, press the right buttons, you can force someone to do what you want. The tactic assumes that the other person is a robot and that only *you* have free will. Manipulative acts—those designed expressly to elicit desired reactions from others—sustain such a view; they make the other person's reaction seem mechanical rather than real, constrained rather than volunteered.

Manipulation always makes other people seem less free, less human, less responsive to your own personal value. You get a sense that the other person is merely doing what he *has* to do. If you manipulate someone, it will seem to you that he would not appreciate you or give you what you want *unless* you use the tactic.

In the examples given, everyone involved loses—even if the device "succeeds." Lisa will always feel shaky with Dan, as if she must pump up his interest in her to keep the relationship going. Even if Dan had intended to call her anyhow, even if he really *wanted* to see her, Lisa can't know this because she didn't allow that possibility. You can see how one manipulation leads to another.

And the mother who called her daughter with mock heart trouble—she too dooms herself to feeling unwanted. If the daughter *does* go to Mexico as planned, the mother will see her leaving as the definitive expression of disdain. If the daughter *stays* in response to the call, the mother, having used this tactic, will feel unwanted anyway since the daughter is only staying under duress.

In the case of the boss, who may look down on his employees anyway, his ability to manipulate them merely confirms to him that they are witless and under his power. He may have fun with the money his business brings in, but *not* with the people he spends his day with.

When you manipulate people, you feel unloved by them

and unlovable generally. Multiply a single instance of manipulation by hundreds, by *tens of thousands* in the case of the habitual manipulator, and you can easily see why he seems so cold and feels so isolated and unloved.

The penalties of manipulation are always worst when you care most about the other person, when it's very important to you that the person *genuinely* likes you or loves you and that whatever he does for you comes from the heart.

The implications of manipulativeness are shown dramatically in the story of the romance between Svengali, the master hypnotist, and the young and beautiful Trilby, an artist's model. Svengali's spell ensnares Trilby, inducing her to leave her fiancé and run off with him. It also transforms her into the finest singer in Europe.

Across the continent she goes, performing over the years to packed houses and receiving superb reviews. Svengali is deeply in love with her, always at her side.

But he senses that something is wrong. Each night he asks her, "Trilby, do you love me?" And each night she replies mechanically, "Yes, I do." However, to the hypnotist, who knows that she is in his power, her answer means nothing. He remains unconvinced and each night, feeling especially sad when she says she loves him, he says to himself, "Only Svengali talking to himself again."

The story ends as Svengali grips his chest in the throes of a fatal heart attack and Trilby *slips from his control.* Lacking even the strength to ask her his sad nightly question and knowing that finally she is free, he hears her whisper, "I love you, Svengali," and in his last moments he realizes that she really does. Dying, he recognizes her love, which his own manipulativeness had deprived him of experiencing over the years.

Thus the Projection Principle explains the high cost of manipulation, which many of us understand intuitively but which is hard to articulate without the Principle.

AXIOM XXVI: To the extent that you *manipulate* others, you doom yourself to exist entirely alone in a world of robots—a sterile land of your own creation.

This is the argument not to engage in manipulation and to let people respond as they wish. Only then can you know that you are truly loved and appreciated for yourself.

How much better off you are with the opposite of manipulation, which is being open with people, letting them know the facts and gambling that they will respond as you'd like them to. Using this approach hardly guarantees that you'll get what you're after; in that respect it's riskier. But honesty assumes that *who you are* merits that the other person give you what you want. To know that you're truly worthwhile to even a small circle of friends and loved ones is preferable to having an army of acquaintances who are ready to rebel as soon as you stop conniving. Only by divesting yourself of manipulations can you enable yourself to feel desired and loved.

PRETENSE

Pretense is a particular kind of manipulation, so common that it deserves special discussion.

There may seem nothing wrong with lying about your age, your income, your education, or any other "harmless" fact in order to make a better impression.

In musical comedy, opera, plays, and movies, there are many charming plots involving two people who meet, each pretending to be something he or she is not. The girl pretends to be a debutante, and the boy says he's an oil baron's son on vacation, when in fact, she's a starving actress and he's a penniless singer. After two hours of complications in which both struggle to keep up the sham, they are simultaneously exposed to each other and discover that they're in love for the *right* reasons anyway. For both the characters and the audience, there's enormous relief in shedding the cloak of fraud. The ending is happy and life-affirming.

But that's fiction. In reality, the minute you start touching up your image and pretending that you are something you are not, you begin a Projection that can put you under enormous pressure—and sometimes destroy a relationship.

For instance, Shirley, looking for a prosperous man to marry, rents an apartment in an exclusive neighborhood that she really can't afford. She wants to convince eligible bachelors that she comes from a fine family herself and that she's on her way up in the business world. She refers to herself as an "account executive" in the public relations firm (where she's really an assistant to two account executives). She rounds out her pretense by exaggerating the amount of time she's spent in Europe, constantly chatting about her membership in a racquet club and an art museum, talking about how she wishes she could go sailing more often, and discussing the rich boys she dropped because they were "too dumb." Luckily for Shirley, her working-class parents live halfway across the country so she doesn't have to produce them.

She hopes that a man from a good background, on his way up in the world, will see her as a natural ally, rejecting other women in favor of one who so easily fits into his social scheme.

Shirley saves up all summer and, on Labor Day weekend, goes to a posh resort where she has heard there are rich eligibles aplenty, taking advantage of one of the last sailing opportunities of the season.

The weekend is a great success for Shirley. Friday night she meets Craig, who is about to be given a seat on the stock exchange by his father. He's a good sailor, has varied interests, and people naturally gravitate toward him. He's relaxed about his money and position. The two of them spend a wonderful day sailing on Saturday, and that evening, Craig teaches Shirley how to play backgammon. Sunday they have brunch, after which Craig must leave because he's promised to visit friends elsewhere.

Is Shirley already in love? She has an anxious fear of losing him, which suggests she cares, at the very least. Reflecting on the weekend, she realizes that Craig had said little about himself. She had done nearly all the talking. (It was brittle, nervous chatter—about her past, her job, her hobbies, her vision of the good life. Really, she might as well have been talking about someone else.)

She's already feeling the pressure of her own pretense, and is starting to project onto Craig the identity of a man on his way up who wouldn't want the real Shirley.

It turns out that Craig lives just across town from Shirley, and it occurs to her to invite him over for dinner. But suddenly she despises her apartment and everything in it. How can she serve dinner to Craig when she has no real family silver, which he's surely used to even at an informal dinner, and her china is second-rate by these new standards? And what about her furniture? None of it is antique! She pictures him coming in and politely enduring an evening with the lower classes. He'd never want to come back.

Shirley does have one trump card: her friend Mimi, whose father bought her a co-op in town. Maybe Mimi would throw a small dinner party for them. Mimi agrees, Craig accepts the invitation willingly, and the evening is fun for everyone—except Shirley. Craig's easy enjoyment of the amenities of Mimi's money, his effortless comfort there, convince Shirley that he will be shocked when he sees her apartment.

Notice that Shirley is looking at herself through what she imagines to be Craig's eyes. She's not truly identifying with Craig but engaging in what psychologists call "projective identification"; part of Shirley's Projection on Craig is that he has this viewpoint that she pictures.

The next week Shirley goes to Craig's home. They sleep together, and he gives every indication of really caring for her. He has little interest in material things (to him the stock market is essentially a game) but likes talking about people and ideas, so she should have reason to feel that what he enjoys about her are her sensitivity, her loyalty, her intelligence, her concern for people—all qualities that she genuinely possesses. But instead, she's terrified. She feels like a spy in a hostile country and imagines that she's on the verge of being found out and deported, if not shot.

When Craig does come to her apartment, she's extremely tense and makes excuses about everything there. Though she's gone into debt to buy new items for Craig's visit, she still feels that the place must look like a hovel to him. Once again, she imagines she's seeing through his eyes, so it looks like a hovel to her, too. She construes every affable statement of Craig's as noblesse oblige. She's sure he's humoring her, but she wouldn't dare accuse him of it.

During the next two months, she feels increasingly fraudulent and unworthy of him. When he's taking care of a family emergency and doesn't call for two days, she's convinced that he has suddenly seen the light and is about to drop her for someone in his own class. Maybe he discussed her with his parents and *they* gave him perspective. When he does call, she tries to make her voice as measured and "upper class" as she can. She's very artificial when they're together. Increasingly, she weeds spontaneity out of her performance so that she can't possibly make a slip. Her friends are all called upon to counsel her on the proper decorum with such a person. She practically makes a study of Mimi's behavior. Every thought in her head, every action with Craig, is defensive.

Shirley has generated a view of herself as utterly unworthy of this man. She has deepened her feeling of personal fraudulence. By her treatment of Craig, she has made him seem stiff, demanding, unfeeling, intolerant—in short, the archetype of a contemptuous aristocrat. She can't possibly have a place with such a man, and trying to squeeze herself into such a niche is agonizing. But still she persists.

By the fourth month, Shirley has lost her sensitivity, her concern, her spontaneity—all the qualities that endeared her to Craig in the first place. When she goes out with his friends, she's so busy striving to appear natural that she asks them nothing about themselves. They don't know who she really is—they only see her anxiety. Believing that Craig is about to drop her, and for good reason, she starts to become jealous and accusatory. She fixates on a wealthy woman friend of Craig's, someone he's known since childhood, and theorizes that Craig and the woman sleep together periodically. "Why shouldn't they? They belong together. They can talk about their trust funds," she muses ironically.

With this full-blown Projection that Craig is looking down on her as a trivial amusement, she finds life unbearable. Her paranoia makes her miserable and she sits up nights wondering what's going to happen next. She's hardly surprised when he tells her, "I like you a lot, but it's not working. I think we ought to see other people." She replies, "I knew all along you felt that way."

After a few days of torment, she is actually relieved that Craig is out of her life. She knew when he spoke that he was letting her down gently. Now all that remains is to pay off the credit card bills for the new furniture and clothing she bought for this romance.

Wherever there is pretense in a relationship, you convince yourself to some degree that pretense is required. For how could you possibly take the trouble to engage in a cover-up if it weren't necessary or useful in your relationship?

AXIOM XXXVII: Every cover-up of a deficiency in yourself, real or imagined, is an accusation of another person that may or may not be correct. The Projection of such acts is that the other person would lower his esteem for you or disown you outright if the truth came out.

Covering up deficiencies is the true cause of *all paranoia,* and the starting place for unwarranted feelings that another person would persecute you if he knew who you really were. Such cover-ups may result in a Projection that's best described as "miniparanoia"—the person who fibs on his job interview and has flashes of fear that the boss may find out and fire him. In other cases, cover-ups lead to paranoid psychosis. The pattern of cover-up increases and the person projects onto others the sense that they are mortal enemies.

The word "projection" first came into use in connection with paranoia. But it's never been really understood that Projections are created by actions. It was thought that paranoia developed as a disease "inside" and that people merely showed symptoms of the illness by the way they acted. In reality, the actions, which stem from incipient fears, both create and enlarge the paranoid Projection.

AXIOM XXXVIII: If you catch yourself being paranoid in any way, look for the pretense underneath. Drop every single action by which you conceal who you really are and, after an anxious period, the Projection will dissolve.

If, at any point, Shirley had dropped all her pretenses and simply been herself with Craig, if she had even gone so far as to express to him her concern about her less privileged background, he would probably have reassured her that it didn't matter. He might even have welcomed the chance to know her better and to prove to her that he loved her for herself alone.

Certainly, her "disadvantage" in social status was far less of a handicap to her relationship than she thought. What turned Craig off was Shirley's artificiality, her general constriction, her obsession with herself, and her self-centered concern over how she was appearing.

LYING AND BETRAYAL

Any untruth—not just pretense—can lock us into a Projection of another person as undesirable or as dangerous.

Perhaps the two main reasons people lie are to avoid blame or recrimination for something they've done, and to make it easier for them to do something forbidden without another person blocking them. Probably no one is exempt from having lied for either of these two reasons.

Lily is married to a man who constantly berates her for even the smallest fault. He's full of "you should have" and "I wish you would." He loves her but he's sanctimonious, especially about his home and possessions. Lily, who runs her mail order business out of their apartment, is tense by nature. Her mother was scrupulous and quick-tempered so, as a child, Lily learned it was more expedient to come up with excuses than to admit mistakes. At the end of each day, Lily automatically cleans up her husband's desk along with her own work area; this cuts down on his complaining about how messy the apartment is when he gets home.

One day Lily knocks over a vase and the water spills, ruining a letter that her husband had spent a few hours writing to his cousin. When he walks in the door, before he even sees the accident, she says that the cat did it. He scowls, but even *he* can't really lecture the cat.

In this way Lily's been playing it safe with him over the years. But let's look at the Projection of him that *she* fosters in her own mind: "He'd go crazy if he knew. God knows what he'd say or how he'd act if I told him *I* did it."

Consider how Lily makes herself more unhappy by sustaining this Projection. She sees her husband as all-powerful. She's convinced herself that the whole world will somehow collapse if he really gets angry with her.

Even though at this moment a direct confrontation might shake her, Lily could regain her happiness and her freedom by creating a crisis—by telling the truth. If she waited until her husband came in and sat down before telling him, rather than rush to forestall his rage, if she then told him simply that it was an accident and she was guilty, he'd either take it in stride or go berserk. But even in the latter case, if she held fast or yelled back, he'd see how irrational he was. In an even worse scenario, if they didn't speak for two days over it, she would be puncturing her Projection, and on her way to repairing their relationship. Even Lily knows, in her saner moments, that her marriage isn't in jeopardy.

AXIOM XXXIX: People who lie to avoid blame or recriminations often die a thousand deaths, when the reality might not bring even one.

Perhaps *you've* been treated with kid gloves and lied to on the assumption that you would go wild if the person told you the truth. When you sensed this was happening, you were very hurt. You felt rotten about being handled that way—about being dealt with as if you were unforgiving and irrational.

How did you *know* that this was going on? Maybe the other person regularly used euphemisms in talking to you:

"I *lent* two hundred dollars to my brother." (In reality, "brother" never repays money and it was a pure gift.)

"The boss *may* drop over Saturday night." (You know perfectly well that the boss is already *scheduled* to come over; the other person is letting you in on the fact by degrees.)

Maybe the person habitually *delays* before telling you questionable news. The worse the news bulletin, the closer to the deadline you get it: "Sorry, darling, we can't go to the country tomorrow afternoon. I have to go the office." (You know that this was really decided days ago.)

Or the person tells you big things very incidentally: "By the way . . ." A soft voice that isn't usually his can be the giveaway; he's trying not to alarm you so you don't smash the furniture.

Sometimes the person is so obvious as to preface his remark by saying, "Now, please don't get furious, but . . ." Or he brings in friends to back up his statements and to embarrass you into responding quietly or at least staying partially under control.

When you spot that another person projects upon you this kind of irrationality and short fuse, follow the rules for stopping any Projection. Spotlight what the person is doing and ask him to stop. If he doesn't, escalate. It's important that you not be seen this way. With such a person, you'll never know if you're hearing the truth or not. In the end, being lied to may bring out every irrational impulse that *is* in you. Ironically, in response to so much "handling," you're inclined to become the very person your handler feels you are.

The other form of lying is motivated not by fear but by expedience.

David lies to his wife, Norma, telling her he has to play golf because he solidifies his business deals on the golf course. Actually, he sees very few business contacts when he plays. For business purposes, he'd be better off in his office, making phone calls. But he thinks that if Norma knew he had leisure time, she'd want to fill it taking him shopping and suggesting home repair projects.

Over twenty years of marriage, David has made it "effortless" for himself to go and play golf, while reaping the extra benefit of Norma's admiring his dedication to the well-being of their home.

David doesn't know a fib from a reality anymore when talking to Norma, but he would never misrepresent his golf score by even one stroke, nor would he lie to his buddies about anything.

True, Norma is a clinging person, but by using this tactic over the years, David has convinced himself that she's a hopeless drag and that she must be lied to if he is to have any freedom in life. In fact, he has convinced himself that a man's role in marriage is to lie to women to keep them happy.

Notice that in the service of this Projection, he has enslaved himself. He has forged his own chains. In reality, David works hard, makes a very good living, takes care of his family, and deserves to have a hobby. He would be a lot better off confronting Norma directly. "Look, dear, I love you, but I enjoy playing golf. It has nothing to do with you or the kids."

If she can't understand this, he might do well to explain that she's making herself a jailor. Why should he have to spend every hour of his life running errands for her, or even in her company? It's very likely that if David insists, Norma will understand that there is no insult intended. Almost surely, she's felt over the years that he didn't want to be with her and was exaggerating the business function of his golf. The truth will set them both free.

AXIOM XL: The habit of lying to people for expedience projects a sense of them as obstacles. You convince yourself that they won't listen to reason and can't change. You make your life unnecessarily complicated.

The penalties are always greatest when you lie in a romance. To project onto a neighbor the notion, "This person must be told what he wants to hear," may not cause great personal deprivation. But to teach yourself that this is true of a person you're in love with is to terminate high romance.

There are many temptations to break the faith with loved ones. In every love relationship, there is an understanding between the partners that goes far beyond what they've ever thought to make explicit. For instance, it's likely to be assumed that you won't talk deprecatingly about your sex life with your mate, or maybe that it's too precious and personal for you to discuss it even favorably. It's likely to be understood that you won't announce your partner's latest financial position or discuss some failing of his that he's very sensitive about and is trying to correct. You won't blame the other person for decisions that both of you made: "Oh, sorry we can't come for the weekend; Neil doesn't feel like seeing anyone." In nearly all serious relationships, it's assumed that you won't flirt with people outrageously or have an affair behind the other person's back.

Violations on any level, whether or not the other person knows about them, injure relationships by adversely affecting your view of the person, making the person less desirable to you. As you gossip about your sex life, you make it less exclusive and romantic. As you talk about your mate's recent financial misjudgment, you're disposing yourself just a little to see him as incompetent and maybe laughable. When you talk about how your mate is trying to overcome a failing, whether it's being too quick-tempered or being too wimpy or whatever, you enlarge in your mind an image of the person as a mental patient and not a lover.

Even asking friends for advice on how to deal with your mate may breach an implied contract. The high romance comes from the two of you working things out together privately.

Betrayal in a relationship, whether it is as subtle as buying something for yourself that you would never buy if the other person were with you or as obvious as having an affair that would devastate the other person if he knew about it, is especially dangerous because the other person is not able to see the acts or to stop them. Each betrayal downgrades the person in your mind and sets the stage for the next. By the time the person realizes what's going on, he may have become so unimportant to you that you won't be prone to heed his objections.

There are many relationships in which one person is scrupulously honest and hopeful, while the other does whatever suits him at the moment. The partner who keeps the faith is constantly reinforcing his happiness with the other person and inducing himself to stay in love. The cheating partner is destroying his love for the other person and, in the end, his own happiness.

Pam trusts her husband, Ted. She believes whatever he says, makes arrangements for their social life, and even helps him in his work. She generates in her own mind the Projection that marriage is for a lifetime and love is eternal. But Ted tells friends, "Pam got married eight years ago, but *I* didn't." He flirts, has affairs, gambles with money they've both agreed to save, and lies to Pam as easily as getting up in the morning. Pam's Projection of loyalty in marriage, fostered by her own behavior, is so strong that it's almost inconceivable to her that Ted could be abusing her.

Ted, on the other hand, has reduced Pam to the role of stay-at-home social secretary and servant. He takes no joy in her at all anymore. In fact, he hates going home. Not only does Pam bore him, but all women seem to him stupid and gullible. He can't have sex more than three times with anyone.

With their contrasting Projections, *Ted* is the one who is finally so unhappy that he asks for the divorce. Afterward he goes on picking up women only to drop them disappointedly, except that now he has no home and no social secretary. Because of her Projection, the divorce is shattering for Pam. She has never done *anything* to devalue Ted or her belief in their relationship. Her Projection of him as the one man in her life remains.

After a few months, friends try to console her by introducing her to eligible men, but she feels paralyzed and disloyal to Ted.

In cases like this, an understanding of the Projection Principle is invaluable. *Just as you can use the Principle to stay in love, you can use it to help yourself fall out of love when you have to.*

Pam must start to do a set of things that amount to "mini-betrayals" of Ted's memory. She must stop defending Ted when friends comment on how terrible he was to her. Instead she must force herself to agree with them when she knows they are right. If there is a money settlement for her and the children, she must ask for her full entitlement and not take less just to show Ted how much she still cares for him. When she goes out on dates, she must make a huge effort not to compare each man with Ted—favorably or unfavorably. Ted must no longer be the yardstick by which she measures others or herself. If she's attracted to a man but her "loyalty" to Ted inhibits her from sleeping with this new person, it's important for her to do what *she* really wants rather than paying homage to a memory. Instead of avoiding the restaurant that used to be their favorite, she must go to it. It would help her to stop talking about Ted, especially avoiding remarks like "Ted used to love that kind of ice cream" or "Ted would really enjoy this show."

Everything that Pam does concerning Ted should absolutely *exclude* the idea of loyalty. If a man she likes asks her about Ted, she should force herself either to be quiet or to hold Ted culpable for what went wrong. She must avoid *any* act of loyalty to Ted that would revive her old Projection of him as the only man in her life and prolong her pain and isolation.

The Projection Principle gives us an understanding of why the memory of certain people stays with us and even grows over time. The same process that enables us to stay in love, to keep romantic visions afloat in our minds, may, if we know how to use it, permit us to banish memories that burn brighter than we want them to. Thus, by using the Projection Principle, we have control even over memories that seem to haunt us in life.

AXIOM XLI: Betrayals of another person, no matter how slight, whittle away the other person's value to you.

If you've been in a relationship and you suddenly begin to feel that, for no apparent reason, the person is seeing you as less worthy or is less in love with you, it's very possible he has been doing things behind your back that have reduced you in his mind. These may have been deliberate deceptions or small, symbolic violations of what he knew you would expect and want.

It's very important that you not try to deny to yourself what looks like slippage in your relationship. It's true that you're up against an especially tough Projection if it's based on betrayals, because they were formed and sustained without your knowledge. But as with all Projections, the earlier you do something, the better, so you ought to say something as soon as you sense the problem.

You may approach it with the same vagueness that you feel: "I get the impression that there's something different about us, Ken. Is there anything that's making you unhappy?" Obviously, you can't ask questions like this regularly without seeming like a paranoid or a nag. That's what makes the intervention so hard. If the person reconsiders, fine. You'll see a change for the better in your relationship. If he doesn't change, you must escalate just as you would in trying to stop any other Projection: "There's clearly something going on in your life, Ken. Or in your head. *I'm* not happy with the way you're speaking to me lately or with the way you seem to want to be away from me as much as possible."

If the relationship is just beginning, you'll probably suggest taking a break at this point or at least slowing down. If it's a long-term relationship or a marriage, you may want to talk about what you feel is being lost and the pitfalls that lie ahead unless something is done. But whether your intervention succeeds or fails, if you act, you won't be a passive victim. At least you'll be trying to combat the unseen abuses, and that will make you feel somewhat better.

AXIOM XLII: If another person seems to be downgrading his opinion of you for no apparent reason, consider the possibility that he may be forming a new Projection of you based on bad treatment of you behind your back. Intervene as you would with any Projection.

INFORMANTS

Whenever you lie, pretend, or betray someone, you give certain people an unholy power to threaten you—or even destroy you. You are creating, out of nothing, the *psychological informant.*

The informant is anyone whose very presence reminds you of the truth, or reveals it.

In some cases, the informant may activate fear in the dissembler because he *knows* that a lie was told, or knows something bearing on the truth that may reveal the lie, even accidentally. Or, if you've pretended something that isn't so, the informant may highlight your limitations. He may jeopardize your disguise by having the real goods. In other cases, the informant may have been a witness to your acts of betrayal. In detective and spy novels, where we see many cases of "the man who knew too much," informants are sometimes murdered because they happened to witness a dark deed—or someone *thought* they witnessed it. In some plots, the informant never would have used the information at all or didn't even know he had it.

But psychological informants also come in a subtler variety. Some people, *by their very existence,* inform against us.

Margot has been miserable in her marriage for many years. In the beginning, she thought about divorce, but felt her biological clock ticking away so she had children instead. She sought to "solidify" her marriage by joining civic groups with her husband, by dragging him to marriage counseling when he didn't want to go, and by insisting that he see a private analyst who would help him "grow up." She knew that he had had a serious affair with a local woman he'd met, and devoted herself to averting a recurrence. She assiduously kept him away from single women. She spent a great deal of time talking to him about the necessity of marriage and responsibility and decrying those who weren't family people. Her life was a massive, exhausting pretense.

She had dull, "good" times with others in the same boat, and sometimes, with compatibly married people in the area. But almost every day she suffered acute pain—she was stabbed by *informants.* These were people whose *very existence* reminded her of her own pretense—of her own lies to herself—and showed her the opposite of her pretense, the possible alternatives to the life she had chosen.

A couple moved in nearby, and the woman said about her partner, "We want to live together for a while *and be really sure* before we get married and have children." Margot felt dizzy when she heard this and lapsed into a lecture that they shouldn't wait too long. In reality, she couldn't stand the idea that anyone had the gumption to resist the pressure to marry fast. Maybe if *she* had done the same thing . . . But morals were stricter fifteen years ago and anyway, it wasn't so safe to have babies in your thirties then. Subsequently, she avoided that couple because they were living reminders of her past mistakes and, worse yet, of her current pretense. Of course the other woman had no idea that in Margot's Projection, she was a dangerous informant.

Phyllis, one of Margot's dearest friends, became an even deadlier informant overnight. Margot had known for a few years that Phyllis was not too happy in her marriage, but had assumed that Phyllis would hang on forever and consider herself lucky to have a man. Once Phyllis had tried to explain to Margot that although her marriage had a lot of good things in it, there were still a lot of bad, concluding, "It really hasn't worked for either of us." Margot told Phyllis she shouldn't talk like that; she should just try to make the best of things, as everyone does. But Margot had no impact. Suddenly, Phyllis announced she was getting a divorce. Here she was, leaving a marriage better than Margot's had ever been, ready to gamble on making her own way, with no more money than Margot would have, and two sons in college. Margot was stricken. Phyllis's decision was like a public declaration that Margot was living a lie, an unnecessary lie—that Margot was a coward. After remonstrating in vain one more time, she could think only of keeping Phyllis away from her own husband, who might get ideas at the very least—as if he didn't know that people ever got divorced.

One person after another in a pretender's life reminds him that his house is built on quicksand. Margot, for example, had as informants people who hesitated before marriage, people who had no interest in marriage, people who broke up marriages, gay people who opted for a different kind of life, and "unconventional" people of all varieties. Moreover, people who enjoyed sex were informants, as were people with *truly happy marriages.* In fact, for Margot, almost everyone she met was an informant; she was hard put to find a protective cadre of people who lived as miserably as she did.

Margot's lie consumed her whole life. But anyone who lies on any level, no matter how small, creates these shadowy informants. Typically, they are people who are behaving honorably where we are behaving dishonorably; people who truly are what we are pretending to be; people who are living happily and successfully in ways that we have ruled out as impossible for ourselves—or anyone.

You've bragged about an ability of yours or an area of expertise. When a real expert comes along, he's an informant. You're living the lie of pretending that you're doing important work of some kind: Your children couldn't do a thing without you, your boss would be lost if you went on vacation. Your child informs against you by growing up and becoming independent, and a "temp" informs against you by taking perfect care of your boss while you're in Europe.

Probably much of the punishment for victimless crimes and much societal condemnation of certain groups is motivated by a hatred of informants: Homosexuals who choose to live without children; women who want sex lives as free as those of men and are capable of handling them; poor people who, in many cases, are as happy as those who've devoted their lives to acquiring wealth.

Because informants may innocently cause so much distress to people whose systems of life (if they were honest with themselves) are not what they would really want if they had more courage, the brutality against informants has been mind-boggling over the ages. Irreligious people have been burned at the stake, women with the guts to fall in love with a man they couldn't marry were turned into pariahs, and as we've all seen, minority group members able to live outside the traditional network are still frequently penalized.

Whenever an innocent person makes you acutely uncomfortable, that person is likely to be an informant. If you find yourself troubled by someone whose performance doesn't warrant your anxiety, withhold criticism of him and examine yourself. Ask in particular, "What is it that *I* might want to do or experience that this person is now doing happily?" "In what way might *I* be masquerading with myself and others, which this person is making me aware of?"

AXIOM XLIII: It's better to use informants to lead us out of the wilderness than to avoid them or seek to destroy them. Indeed, informants in your life, if you spare them and listen to them, can be among your best instructors.

GIVING

The act of giving to others provides a good illustration of how an act's *motivation* determines its *Projection.* People give for different reasons, which foster very different pictures of those they give to.

For instance, you may be giving to another person because you feel inferior and are compensating for what you consider to be a deficiency of yours. You may give in order to obligate another person, consciously or unconsciously. You may give purely out of the fear that people will walk out on you if you don't keep delivering. You may give as a show of self-abnegation, the way a martyr does. Or you may give in a pure, free, generous vein with your only aim being to enhance the other person.

In each case, the Projection formed or sustained by the act of giving is utterly different, and your relationship may take a very different course as a result.

Jeanette is a talented interior decorator who has just gone back to work after the dissolution of a long marriage. People love what she does for their homes and recommend her highly. If she'd just calm down, she'd have a fantastic business in no time. But she has it in her head that she's been away from the business world so long that she'd better not press her luck—she'd better "give" as much as she can to her clients. She charges too little when she could command much higher fees, and she rarely takes more than one job at a time, afraid that she won't be able to give her clients the attention they deserve.

Her giving is especially off base with Emma, a super-rich widow whose country home Jeanette recently redecorated. Emma is thrilled with Jeanette's work, likes her very much, and has taken a personal interest in finding other clients for her, saying, "I'm doing my *friends* a favor telling them about you."

But all this praise makes Jeanette feel shakier than ever. Has she deluded Emma? Jeanette begins to fear that she never *really* comes through for Emma, that she's done less than Emma imagines, and that she's opened Emma up to embarrassment if visitors come and see that the job lacks professional touches.

Nearly every week she gets some new idea about the "completed" country home and asks if she can drive the sixty miles out there to make some improvement, at no extra cost. Emma finds it impossible to discourage such giving or even to pay Jeanette for some items which Jeanette insists on throwing in for nothing. Since Emma is taking such an interest in Jeanette's life, Jeanette feels that she must do everything she can think of for Emma. She spends a whole day searching bookstores for a cookbook Emma mentioned wanting to own.

All this giving on Jeanette's part, which is motivated by her own self-doubt and the terrible dread that Emma will find out and be disappointed, has very deleterious effects on Jeanette. Her Projection of Emma, instead of that of "true friend," is that of "scrupulous client" who, though generous, expects a flawless, superlative performance at all times. With this Projection, she can't believe even Emma's most sincere praise. Or in moments when she *does* believe that Emma is sincere, it seems to her that Emma must not be too bright or sophisticated in matters of design.

Jeanette's Projection also makes life harder for Emma, who at sixty is only slightly older than Jeanette. Emma is indifferent to social status and would love to become better friends with Jeanette. She's a bit lonely, and she and Jeanette share many interests. She feels put off when Jeanette keeps treating her like an employer and turns down invitations to her home. It's as if Jeanette *wants* an imbalance in the giving, and Emma feels cheated and estranged by that imbalance. Jeanette refuses to allow Emma the pleasure of giving to a graceful recipient. A real relationship never develops.

When you give to indebt a person, your Projection is that the person *wouldn't* do your bidding if you didn't give, but *must* come through as long as you keep priming the pump. In many cases you convince yourself that the person cares much less for you than he really does, forcing yourself into unnecessary sacrifices.

There are people who give too much to a particular person for a lifetime, making themselves miserable to coerce another person to love them. At the end, when they're disabled or dying, they may find out that the other person felt smothered by the giving, and saw their true motive all along. Or, in some cases, they discover that the other person truly loved them, would have loved them with or without the "overgiving," and is glad to be able to repay their lifelong concern. In short, giving to obligate people seldom succeeds in its purpose, but always makes you feel worse.

We've all seen marriages where one person makes ridiculous sacrifices in fear that the other person will walk out. And we've all seen parents, lovers, and even friends who give to excess in order to proclaim their selflessness and worthiness.

The ideal act of giving, of course, is when you simply want the other person to benefit from what you give: comfort, empathy, reassurance, advice, physical help, money. The Projection of such giving is your view of the other person as "precious," as "beloved," as "worth giving to."

Only in connection with this last form of giving would you be totally ready to give anonymously: the way most parents would to children, most lovers would to each other, and most pet owners would to their cats or dogs. Such giving is not a tactic, but a natural expression of feeling, a fundamental way of enabling us to keep caring about another person and seeing him as desirable.

SUMMARY

The Projection Principle can help you to understand the real impact of nearly any tactic you employ in relationships.

When you manipulate others, you make it impossible for yourself to feel loved by them. You turn people into nothing more than robots responding to your push-button techniques—dooming yourself to a feeling of isolation.

When you use pretense of any kind to "improve" a relationship, you make it seem that other people are intolerant and would reject you if they knew the "real" you. Cover-ups and the denial of reality are the starting place for producing paranoid Projections. It's important to screen for such behavior and drop it as soon as you recognize it.

Lying and betrayal always downgrade the other person in your own mind. You can destroy your belief in people, your respect for them, or your love of them without their having any idea of what's happening. Therefore, if you even suspect that someone is treating you dishonestly behind your back, it's crucial that you confront the person at once, or it will be too late.

Every dishonest concealment of a flaw creates in your own mind "informants"—people whose very presence reminds you of the reality. You imbue such people with the power to cause you acute distress. You would do far better to study that distress and attempt a remedy than to keep banishing informants from your life.

Even such a seemingly straightforward act as giving to others may, depending upon your outlook when you give, cause any of a wide variety of Projections. Giving for the wrong reasons can distance you from another person or even destroy a relationship; giving as a genuine expression of feeling can enhance your view of the other person and solidify your relationship.

10

PROJECTIONS
IN THE OFFICE

Y ou may spend a major part of your life at work, perhaps in an organizational setting. There you either express yourself freely and creatively, feeling at home, or your job is a pressure cooker and you count the minutes until you can escape.

Whether you are primarily a boss or an employee, a great deal of your success in business and much of your daily happiness depends on how *you* see your job and how *others* see you. Certainly, in every job there are some things you can't control: company policies, demands of workload, the pay scale, and the occasional recalcitrant person whom no one will ever change. But with what you now know about the Projection Principle, you can exert much more control over your fate in the office than you might have imagined—over how you feel about going to work each day and how you are treated once you get there.

It may not have occurred to you that *you* can influence whether you're given plum assignments, invited to meetings, promoted, treated with deference, or asked for advice. But all these things and more depend upon how people see you, and the Projection Principle shows that you *do* have considerable input into this.

Naturally you also have input into how *you* see others, and how you see the work experience. Even events that seem insignificant, interactions with people that last only moments, can start Projections going for you and for others.

In this chapter, we'll be looking first at how *you* can keep a healthy involvement with your work and the people you deal with, and then at several types of interactions that influence how others see you.

YOUR OWN
HEALTHY OUTLOOK

Greg, a recent Princeton graduate, competent and ambitious, began working in a big New York law firm. He was awestruck by its prestige (which had been reinforced all through school), by its size and the huge sums of money the firm billed and handled, and by the luxury of the place itself: its plush carpets, antique furniture, and state of the art equipment. Greg, who came from a small town, found it overwhelming that the office was open twenty-four hours a day and that notary publics were there at three o'clock in the morning.

He joined a bevy of workers who did legal research and

toiled away for three months without even seeing any of the senior partners whose pictures hung on the wall.

Late one Friday afternoon, four months into the job, Greg suddenly realized that he was hungry and exhausted. He'd been doing complicated research since early morning, and the small print of the precedent cases he'd been poring over was starting to run together. He decided he needed a break. Greg felt it would take too long to order a sandwich from the local luncheonette, so he just reached into his briefcase and found a big chocolate bar he had bought that morning. He got a cup of coffee from the office machine and relaxed at his desk with a newspaper, munching his candy bar while reading the sports section.

Just then the door opened. Lo and behold, it was Sidney G., the most renowned partner, right there in the Research Department! Greg recognized him instantly from his portrait in the board room.

In a flash, Greg thought, "Oh no, after all my work, now he comes in when I've got a newspaper and a chocolate bar. How can I get rid of them? I can get fired for this. But he hasn't seen them yet."

As his mind was thus churning, Greg's hands were groping under his desk, shoving the contraband materials back into his briefcase.

Passing behind Greg, Mr. G. asked casually, "Young man, Lydia didn't leave yet, did she? I need her to sign a deposition." Lydia was Greg's immediate supervisor.

"No sir," Greg replied at once. "I've been here at my desk working all day, and I didn't see her walk out. She must be in her office."

By the time Greg finished his sentence, Mr. G. was almost out of earshot. Afterwards Greg didn't feel right about retrieving his snack or going back to the newspaper, and so he tried to resume his research, but it was hard not to keep replaying his exchange with the super-boss.

As the minutes ticked by it seemed more and more likely to Greg that Mr. G. *had* seen the newspaper and the candy and, worse yet, had seen Greg trying to conceal the evidence. And what did Mr. G. mean by saying, "Lydia didn't leave yet, did she?" Maybe he phrased the question that way to show how shocked he'd be if anyone left early on a Friday afternoon or shirked their responsibilities. If so, it was *certainly* directed at Greg. Then Greg noticed something *really* terrible: his coffee cup! "Mr. G. *must* have seen this. And I said I was at my desk all day. Now he'll *know* I was lying. He'll realize I must have left my desk to get the coffee." Greg had a troubled weekend.

Within a few moments, Greg had acted in two ways that started a Projection of Sidney G. as unreasonable, demanding, without empathy, and watching each employee narrowly.

The first of these actions was, of course, hiding his "illicit" recreations. Because Greg acted out of fear, out of a belief that the boss *might* be unreasonable, he *intensified* that view. He somewhat confirmed his suspicion that if Sidney G. had seen him eating at his desk, the senior partner would have been seriously dissatisfied and would not have reasoned that the snack was taking the place of Greg's lunch. Observe that by his own act, Greg "confirmed" something to himself, though there was no outside evidence for it whatsoever.

Greg's second paranoia-inducing act was his camouflage statement that he'd been at his desk continuously. Why would he need such a ruse if it were not that Sidney G. thought he was running a sweatshop? Thus, Greg's very cover-up confirmed his fear. Worse yet, it led to another nightmare concept: that Sidney G., in running his sweatshop, had developed an ability to see into the very thoughts of his slaves. Ironically, the pretense introduced into Greg's mind the notion of his own transparency.

The next week Greg made it his business to study Lydia's comments, and even her facial expressions, to see if perhaps Sidney G. had complained to her about Greg's delinquency. Greg couldn't put his finger on anything in particular. But then, such a skilled professional as Lydia wouldn't reveal what she was thinking. On the premise that he *might* be in trouble, Greg spent a little more time cultivating Lydia, getting in a few remarks about how much work he took home.

Greg became fanatical about getting in earlier than Lydia, and staying later, even cancelling a dinner date once to outlast his supervisor. He took to quoting to Lydia the tiniest compliments that he'd received from other lawyers, and referred several times to his Phi Beta Kappa standing. When Lydia had other things on her mind, Greg took her indifference as a statement: "I know what you're doing and I don't like it."

Greg's status in the firm was really secure, but he didn't know it. He felt he must be sinking.

After another eight weeks, Greg had generated a true paranoid state. He felt persecuted, transparent, unwanted. He had Projected onto Lydia and his other bosses a collective stringency that made life in the firm almost unbearable. He began looking for another job, figuring that he would need one very soon.

Paranoia is, by far, the chief organizational illness. Anyone who works in a contained environment and needs that environment for his security becomes prone to it. By acting on the potentiality of danger, you can very easily blow up the Projection that other people are against you, or don't need you, or maybe even that they have already found your replacement.

The art of working in any organization is to stay honest, as open as you hope you are in your personal life. Deal with your colleagues and bosses fairly but fearlessly. Treat them, above all, *as if they are reasonable;* then if individuals prove otherwise, you can confront them or make some adjustment, or perhaps even leave the setting in favor of another one. It may be hard, but you will have the best career success, you will foster the best Projections *on* yourself, and the best Projections *for* yourself on others, if you force yourself to act with your business associates as if you don't *need* them for survival.

You have available the option of creating and sustaining a healthy Projection on your bosses and fellow workers, and of encouraging *them* to form a healthy Projection on you.

Suppose Greg had allowed himself to be "discovered" snacking and relaxing at his desk. Suppose he had refused to defend himself for something he knew wasn't a crime. Instead of convincing himself that Sidney G. was a heartless slave driver, he would have been his the way to seeing Sidney G. as a normal person whose high-order intelligence permitted him to recognize normal situations for what they were. He would have felt at home in the firm and hopeful of advancement. If it had turned out, by some fluke, that Sidney G. *was* a maniac boss, at least Greg would have known that he himself was doing more than his share and that he was dealing with a nut. He would have preserved his sense of how he *ought* to be treated.

Meanwhile, in all likelihood, Sidney G. was too busy to notice Greg one way or another.

AXIOM XLIV: Keeping up your own healthy Projections on your boss, employees, and co-workers is essentially a matter of staying honest and not letting fear motivate you and convince you that your job is undesirable.

To guard against going wrong, it will certainly help to make a list of any behaviors that you engage in out of fear and the sense that another person *might* be trouble. The true path is to resist those behaviors and simply allow others to be at their best or at their worst, while you stay on course and deal with each contingency only when it comes along.

But business life is more complicated when it comes to *exerting impact over other people's picture of you.* Nearly everything people do influences the way they see you: even the most innocent acts do more than *express* a perception; they *intensify* ideas people hold about you and congeal those ideas into full-blown Projections. Therefore, it isn't enough to be good at what you do; it's also important to keep people's view of you on the right track.

HOW YOU
LOOK TO OTHERS

Much that goes wrong in the office may seem like "bad luck." People just don't seem to appreciate who you are or what you can do. Perhaps you feel that you've never had a chance to demonstrate your skills, or that when you were really operating at your best, no one was watching.

As marketing manager reporting to Ernie S., marketing director, Laura learned every procedure, where every piece of paper was, and the name of every contact in twenty-six major cities. She handled sensitive situations under pressure: smoothing out shipping problems for the sales department, getting cooperation from touchy department heads, and ministering to irascible customers. People often said that she was the "soul" of the place, that nothing would work without her.

She was delighted for Ernie when he moved on to a much bigger job elsewhere, though she knew she'd miss him personally. At Ernie's big going-away bash at a swank hotel, she cried when Ernie announced that he could never have done his job without her.

Heir apparent to Ernie's job? That would be an understatement. Laura had been *doing* the job and, as everyone knew, she'd been doing it well.

But as the weeks wore on after the big party, no one said anything to Laura about a promotion. In fact, no one mentioned anything to her at all about filling Ernie's spot. As she waited, Laura started having dark suspicions that she might not get the promotion she so obviously deserved. But who else was there? A few possible rivals within the company came to mind. They were capable enough, but no one even came close to knowing the daily routines as Laura did. Maybe top management was recruiting outside the company.

When the announcement finally came, Laura was devastated. Felicia Wanderer. Of all people! She was head of product development at a much smaller firm, had never even *done* marketing before, and was known to be imperious with her staff. Few of the major customers had even *heard* of her! Management had *really* decided to take a chance this time. Felicia had the reputation of being very sophisticated but a prima donna who asked for things and always got them.

There was nothing Laura could say. And even if she *could* make a real argument, who would listen? What could she do—go into the President's office and tell him she was broken-hearted? Could she tell him that he had chosen a woman who probably didn't even give a damn about the company and was just out for herself? Or that he could have gotten Laura for half the money? Of course there would be no point in any of that. Laura could only hope that the president would find out how wrong his choice was within a few months.

Obviously, Laura had no idea of how she was viewed

within her company. Over the years, she had allowed people—bosses and her co-workers alike—to treat her in ways that made them see her as "just a little secretary." In an effort to be diplomatic, she had allowed department heads to blame her and let off steam when they talked to her. She had always welcomed advice, even from those who were in no position to give it and knew less than she did. She thanked people effusively for compliments, even those that were barely disguised insults. She would allow herself to be interrupted from any task or any conversation if the interrupter managed to sound urgent. When anyone accused her of a blunder, she readily apologized and began defending herself, as though it were always open season on her. Thinking the number of friends she had in the company would be crucial, she socialized too much at out-of-town conferences and company parties, even allowing certain company loud mouths to make sexual innuendoes at her expense.

Not wanting to be seen as "difficult," she rarely asked for better treatment, booking herself into inferior accommodations at meetings so the sales force could have the best rooms, and not objecting to anything from small raises in "lean years" to being stuck with an office much too small for her own needs.

Felicia Wanderer, on the other hand, had enjoyed her title of "prima donna," because with it came big jobs, bonuses, a sizable office, and first-class travel accommodations. There was a famous story of Felicia throwing a tantrum because she had to take a plane "too late" at night, and demanding that a car with a driver be at the airport when she arrived. Wherever Laura employed self-abnegation, Felicia took care of herself, pushing her requirements to the very limits. Even though the two were about the same age, people somehow assumed that Felicia was much older than Laura.

Let's leave aside the matter of merit and compare the firm's Projections of Laura and Felicia.

People had given Laura so many orders, so much advice, she had allowed them to second-guess her so often on what she'd done without Ernie that she was seen as unable to make decisions. It made no difference to anyone that she'd been effective one time after another. By their treatment of her, stinting her in so many ways, they had formed and frozen a Projection of Laura as an adequate assistant, but nothing more than that. That's what she was to them, and that's what she would remain. Because they had never treated her as an equal, they simply couldn't appreciate her real worth.

Those in the company knew that Felicia was less informed about procedures than Laura was and even that she was less dedicated. But they wanted someone "upscale," someone with a commanding presence, someone magically creative. They thought that Felicia would be all of these things, an asset to have on their side. They had a Projection of her as decisive, as always getting the best, and as deserving it. They figured that Laura, the reliable "little secretary" could fill "the star" in on details.

Few in the company had actually met Felicia; most knew her only by reputation. They'd had no chance to downgrade her to themselves by treating her badly or withholding anything from her. Because they'd heard that she was a prima donna, she was dealt with almost deferentially during her interviews and salary negotiations. From the first moment, the big bosses elevated her in their own minds by their actions and considered themselves blessed when she took the job.

Just as animals do among themselves, people grapple to establish a hierarchy. When individuals put into any collective situation are forced to deal with each other as in a pack, small acts are used to establish an implicit order. Some individuals gain ascendancy while others lose status. Animals, in their kingdom, use shows of force, real and symbolic; people do things, ranging from the evident to the super-subtle, that cause others to project on them "superior" or "inferior."

MAKING DEMANDS

Every successful business person knows that making demands has a double value. It's not only what you get, but the fact that in granting your requests, your bosses are elevating their respect for you and forming a Projection of you as "entitled."

The trick to making demands effectively lies in pushing to the very *limits* of what you can get, and in never asking for what you know will be *refused* to you.

You might ask for a big office, first-class business travel, a raise, a bonus, a title, an assistant, a larger expense account, certain authorization rights. In fact, you *must* ask for these things if others at your level have them, or if you feel that they are reasonable and your worth to the company merits your having them. Once you are granted what you asked for, people will be quick to justify their giving in. The law of consonance will take over and your bosses will think of you as worth what you got and more. They may start adding other benefits of their own accord.

Not to ask for the very limit of what you deserve is to invite the law of economy to take over. Having given you less and having seen that they won't lose you, management will be inclined to cut even more corners in dealing with you.

"Since Carl didn't complain when we gave his office to that new computer guy, he's probably the best one to exclude from the California sales meeting. After all, we don't have much money this year, and we need somebody to man the phones at home. Carl won't give us any trouble; he knows himself that he doesn't have the status of the others who'll be there."

But recall the danger in being repeatedly refused. If you make a habit of asking for things that your particular company or your particular boss considers outrageous, you will ultimately be viewed as a pest, someone to be turned down. Use your own common sense to determine the likelihood of getting what you want.

However, don't limit yourself only to sure things. And don't be put off if you think that getting something will be a tough battle, or that after you get it you will face some resentment. Doubtless, the first time Felicia Wanderer asked for something only a "prima donna" would receive—maybe her first big bonus—she wasn't sure she'd get it, and she infuriated a few people when she did. But "nothing succeeds like success," which statement is itself a canny insight into the projective process. Bonuses came more easily later because Felicia seemed to merit them. It also began to seem natural for management to picture Felicia with other perks.

Had Felicia been refused outright in her first big request, she would have done well to wait a while before making another such request, and to pick her opportunity carefully. She would need to avoid being seen as "someone to refuse."

ADVICE

Obviously it's better to ask for advice when you need it than to make a major mistake.

On the other hand, every time a person tells you how to do something, if there's even a hint of the notion that you're incompetent, his very act of telling you enlarges that notion in his mind. Habitual advice seekers, people without convictions, don't realize the cost of their repeatedly asking some higher-up or someone on their level how to do a thing.

"Do we number the pages in the center or on the upper right?"

"Will the photocopier work if I don't push this button?"

"Does the boss like to have his mail sorted three times a day or is once enough?"

Pretty soon these eternal questioners exasperate people, and every answer costs them a little more in reputation.

Don't ask advice if you can figure out the answer yourself. And never ask for advice as a form of idle chatter or as a way to break the ice with someone. The other person may respond animatedly and seem to be glad to tell you what you need to know, but he'll think of you as needy, a little less than average, a student, certainly not someone to promote. It's true that if you manage to make a boss notice you, he may even learn your name well ahead of those of other people who started the same day you did. You may feel good about this, but you shouldn't. There's a great deal to be said for being "invisible," for appearing to do your job effortlessly. When someone is to be chosen for a critical assignment under deadline pressure, the boss will remember the quiet, independent person who seemed to figure everything out and "just handle it." Save your visibility for times when it will profit you, such as when you ask for a bigger office or a bonus. Don't waste it asking for advice or reassurance.

Even when you *really need* an answer, think twice about *whom* you ask. Go outside the company if you can. Call a friend who might have the information. Even retain an expert to give you lessons if the advice you need is complex. If you must stay within the company, first go to a co-worker or even a member of your own staff with whom you have a warm relationship. Take your boss's time only as a last resort; avoid encouraging his Projection of you as someone who leans on others.

Truly successful people overprepare for any job. They're careful to ask their bosses only what they need to know and can't find out elsewhere. They make sure that they ask each question only once, which may require having a notebook or tape recorder handy. Anything to reduce the number of times that others feel called upon to take care of them.

The giver of advice has a natural ascendancy over the person who receives it. It's important to know this so that you can recognize those situations when advice is a blatant insult that will downgrade you and hurt your image. You may be familiar with a company "nudge" who makes the rounds of his colleagues' offices, bringing suggestions of what they should *really* be doing.

"I think I've discovered what's wrong with your department . . ."

"You know what you always forget in your presentations? . . ."

"I've been thinking about you at home and I'm worried about you because . . ."

This character is simply irksome when he pops in alone with his "improvements." But he becomes treacherous when he bestows his advice on you in front of a crowd. Others may assume that you need his advice, or even that you ask him for it and depend on him as a matter of routine.

Spotlight what he's doing with humorous exaggeration: "Mario, you're a world-champion advice-giver. That's the seventh helpful correction you've offered me this week." Then, just drop it. If he comes back at you with another helpful hint, tell him, "That's the eighth." If he hits you with another one, escalate. Warmly refer to his compulsion to give advice.

The real tragedy comes on the rare occasion when he *does* have something constructive to say. He's *bound* to hit the right note sometime. Whether you've already reached the same conclusion independently, or a sense of duty makes you feel you must take the advice even though it's *his,* just expect that for a few days he'll take credit for saving your department, maybe even your job. Once again, a little exaggeration of what he's doing will call attention to it: "I would have been utterly lost without you, Mario. I probably would have been fired, and then I would have had to shoot myself."

When *you* are called upon to give advice, remember Mario. Steer clear of giving advice in public and of talking down to anyone who needs your help. If you give unobtrusive support, others will be glad you exist and will respond in kind.

COMPLAINING

In the organization, complaining is the favorite pastime of little knots of losers who band together at lunch to sound off. It is essentially parallel play, with each hearing his own laments and no one particularly caring about those of the others. There may be a show of commiseration, as if to say "I agree with you, now agree with me." But there's little loyalty among complainers. Complaining has nothing to be said for it beyond the fact that it may feel good at the time. Like drinking when you're miserable, it may bolster you temporarily, but in the end it demoralizes you further, aggravating your sense of helplessness. Griping about your job, your salary, your office, your vacation schedule, your fringe benefits, your boss, or your fellow workers makes you feel that nothing you can do will improve your lot and that you are up against impossible odds.

Worse yet, others come to view the chronic complainer as an incompetent who's trying to rationalize his failures. People's desire for consonance makes them want to *believe* that the world is orderly, and to *disbelieve* the complainer: "Al's been whining all week about not getting an assistant. But don't you think there has to be a reason why he *didn't?*"

Karen, on the other hand, says she's being treated wonderfully. Then the response is "Karen must be terrific; they're doing so well by her!"

Not only are complainers often infantile and unpleasant to be around; they are pathetically misguided. The complainer is announcing his self-centeredness and declaring the delusion that other people, fellow workers with problems of their own, will throw their concerns aside to minister to him.

Others almost invariably react to the complainer first with pity and then with contempt. Feeling sorry for him at the start, they may console him as one of life's long-shot unfortunates. However, consoling anyone as a matter of course engenders disrespect for him and reaches the overdose stage quite quickly. Before long most people avoid the complainer and their avoidance stamps in the Projection that he's burdensome and a loser. Thus the sight of the complainer becomes a stimulus for commiseration or flight, both of which renew in people's minds disdain for him and his abilities.

The employee, like the lover, who makes it a rule never to complain but to either ask directly for what he wants or be silent—and if necessary to go elsewhere—will never go wrong.

INTERRUPTIONS: YOURS AND THEIRS

The danger of interruptions, whether you are the interrupter or the regular victim of interrupters, is that they can *trivialize* you or even make you look like a frivolous, or out-of-control character.

Interruptions always connote a feeling of urgency. If you're *urgent* as a matter of course, then you don't have things under control.

Louis, the office manager of a paint supply company, constantly rushes into meetings saying he has to speak to somebody there at once. There's a buyer on the phone, and he needs an answer immediately. The first time he popped into a meeting, a few employees thought he was important. But now, his histrionics in the conference room are a joke.

Louis has *many* interruptive habits. If an invoice is lost, he runs around the office disrupting people and asking them to riffle through their papers, "just in case." When someone is talking to him his eyes often wander, and he frequently says, "Hold that thought while I get a cup of coffee." He lights a cigarette at critical moments, breaking up people's thought processes, as if he dreaded continuity.

Almost no one in the company can put their finger on why they feel so unhinged by Louis's presence, or why they have a picture of him as chaotic and coming apart at the seams. The boss himself, who is a nice guy but a non-psychologist, has no idea why Louis rattles him so badly since Louis does his job fairly well. The universal Projection on Louis is that of a man doing his best against overwhelming odds. Needless to say, Louis would not be the boss's choice as a successor.

Most people resist Louis, but a few women in the organization drop everything when he comes by with his demands. They've always been taught that women should be interruptible. Presumably, they saw their mothers rush to attention when Daddy came home and needed his newspaper. These women, who allow themselves to *be* interrupted, are declaring themselves *subservient.* Other people, seeing how easily Louis can puncture their day, emulate the tactic, thinking of these women as available as needed. By treating them badly, following Louis's example, many in the office project on these women "servant," "second-class citizen," "unpromotable assistant."

The interrupter is unconsciously conveying his anxiety to others in the room. Their Projection of him is that of "disruptive agent," and "enemy to growth." They back away automatically, without identifying his malaise and, in so doing, their picture of him as an undesirable becomes stamped in.

Resist interrupters and, if necessary, spotlight what they're doing: "Please try to be patient, Louis, I'm on the phone."

If you suspect yourself of being an interrupter, study how you feel when you *want* to interrupt someone. Instead of giving into the urge, ask yourself, "Why am I uncomfortable at this moment?" "Am I feeling inferior?" "Is the present subject matter painful to me?" "Am I trying to change the subject because I'm afraid I did something wrong?" "Am I jealous of the person talking, of the attention he's getting, or the success he's reporting?"

A good replacement for the habit of interrupting is the discipline of keeping quiet when the other person is speaking and for a moment afterward. Rather than jump right in as soon as he's finished, or before, rephrase what he has just said. That will show him that you are on his track, and will help keep you there.

COMPLIMENTS

Compliments are among the subtlest of all acts in the human repertoire, and nowhere more so than in the business world. For instance, the person who praises you for traits that required no effort on your part and are unrelated to job performance may actually be disparaging you.

A woman drudges to get a report in on time, and her boss reads it and comments, "You look lovely today." Is he avoiding reference to her work? Possibly. If so, his complimenting her may express contempt for her and will engender more of it in his mind. She should take umbrage and ask outright, "But what do you think of the *report?*"

Our sense of worth springs from our appraisals of those qualities in ourselves over which we have control, those traits that we labored to develop: humanity or integrity, for example. To be given repeated praise for coincidences of life, such as being beautiful or tall or having red hair, is like being given food we can't digest.

We've all felt in bloom after a lovely compliment. But what can make compliments so dangerous is that their very beauty leaves us prey to them. The person who praises us enlarges his own sense of us as needing his praise and being dependent on him and, unless we're careful, we can fall right into the trap. If we ennoble the person to make it seem that he really knows what he's talking about, we belittle ourselves in the process.

Think about the person on your own level who compliments you repeatedly, as if he were your boss.

Caroline is highly competitive with Jane; she wants Jane to think that she has better standing with the top brass than Jane does. She constantly compliments Jane. Jane habitually thanks Caroline for these compliments and even befriends her by showing her a memo she has written before going public with it. But this is exactly what Caroline, in her connivance, wants. Caroline's repeated praise of Jane and Jane's smiling acceptance as she gobbles up the compliments befits a relationship between boss and employee. Caroline, by her use of compliments, is projecting onto Jane the identity of "needy employee." Jane, by thanking Caroline and by her implied dependence on Caroline's judgment of her work, is making herself feel like a child and Caroline's inferior.

Compliments used in such a way amount to a deadly form of arrogance.

Instead of thanking Caroline for what is, in essence, talking down to her, Jane would do well to respond in a very different way when Caroline praises her: "Don't be so proud of me, Caroline, as if I came from nowhere. We're on the same level!"

She might appreciate Caroline's opinion, but ask her to delete personal evaluation. Certainly, she should not curry favor with Caroline by showing her memos she has written. If Caroline refuses to give up her little device, Jane should go further, bringing the problem out in the open: "Thanks, Caroline. But you don't have to compliment me every time I do something. I'm not working for you."

It's a little tougher when Caroline pulls her stunt in front of the full staff. Jane conceives of a plan for handling accounts in the midwest and presents it at a meeting. She is especially hoping that the national sales director and the comptroller will like it; she respects them both so much. But before they can even assimilate the plan, Caroline jumps in and says, "Jane, you did a very nice job. I'm very impressed." Caroline is trying to make it appear publicly that she's Jane's superior—in knowledge and experience if not in rank.

Obviously Jane's got to thank her, but she can do so perfunctorily. She might then turn to those who really count and ask for their opinions, essentially disregarding

Caroline. If she does this deftly, showing that she's neither enraptured and dependent, nor hostile to Caroline, she is, in effect, saying to the others that Caroline was playing a game and trying to usurp their role.

Of course, most people give compliments for genuine reasons, and you should hardly go through life looking for ulterior motives when someone speaks well of you. Usually, gracious acceptance is called for. It's hurtful to the other person if you shrug off a warmly offered compliment as though the giver were too easily impressed or taken in.

Compliments are an intrinsic part of all satisfying relationships. It's not just that *you* enjoy the compliment. Your boss, your co-worker, your staff member, *anyone* who genuinely praises you for something you did further persuades himself that you are worthwhile and deserve to be praised. In most cases, you should encourage other people to solidify their favorable views of you by complimenting you.

A great many people are afraid to compliment others; they fear looking amateurish or gullible, as if complimenting someone is tantamount to saying, "Gee, I've never seen anything like that before!" They fear embarrassment if the other person is unresponsive or says something off-putting like, "Oh, come on, I do that all the time." Also they worry that the other person will get a swelled head and push them around. But the exact opposite is true. When you compliment someone, that person becomes disposed to think of you as recognizing true merit. He would *like* to think that he's doing a good job and you are telling him that he is. He may make you his arbiter, elevating you in his mind. Not that you should use compliments the way Caroline did—as a trick—but you should realize that complimenting someone can actually make you a force. And you yourself will feel the surge of your own influence on others.

ACCUSATIONS

The simple rule for accusations is *never make them.* They're the quickest way to create enemies for a lifetime. People who stand accused by you may not rebut you openly, but will smart over what you've said, possibly forever. If you're in a position of authority, those you accuse, and others, afraid that they'll be next, will form what amounts to an underground resistance to you. They will tend to cover up each other's mistakes, as well as their own, and mass together defensively forming a Projection of you as someone to be dreaded and shunned. Even if they say nothing, these people will wait for you to fall, seizing on any ambiguous situation to make you look bad.

When you accuse people on your level or above you of blunders that denigrate them, you're asking for trouble. You won't have to wait long for a resistance movement to form. Get it out of your head that you'll advance yourself by putting others down. This ploy virtually always backfires by causing others to form a Projection of you as a troublemaker and very likely incompetent yourself. Blaming people for your own mistakes is, of course, the quickest way to go down the drain.

When your job function calls for you to point out a mistake, take the person aside and speak to him without anyone else present. Make clear at the beginning of the conversation that this is between the two of you and that you're going no further with what you're about to say. Don't speculate about *why* the person made the error. Suggest the better alternative. Assuming the person doesn't repeat the mistake, stick to your promise and never mention it again—to him or to anyone else. You can make a friend for life instead of an enemy.

When *you're* accused, first of all determine if you're at fault. If you are, admit the error. Rephrase what the person has said in correcting you so that he will know that you've heard him and that you will amend the faulty behavior. You can turn a near-defeat into a victory by showing class when a real mistake is pointed out to you. People's Projection of you will be that you are flexible and open and that you're sure enough of yourself and your performance to admit mistakes and not feel broken by criticism.

It's trickier to handle those accusations that are true in content but wrong in presentation.

For instance, Doug blundered and forgot to write an important letter in time to meet a deadline. His boss accused him of trying to sabotage the department and of not caring how the boss looked to top management. "If you want my job, one thing's for sure: you won't get it by fouling me up!" Doug was abashed by his own mistake, so he was speechless when the boss delivered this indictment in a full staff meeting. A few commiserated with Doug afterwards, but it did no good. He felt that he'd been wrong and that he'd just have to take whatever the boss dished out.

From that day on, the boss fostered a Projection of contempt for Doug. Having flogged him in public once, it was easier to do it again. He gave Doug some impossible assignments and excoriated him for failing to complete them. Doug became a nervous wreck and three months later quit the job.

Doug had felt so guilty that he had failed to see that the punishment did not fit the crime. True, he'd made a mistake, but he had not done so in bad faith. When he'd discovered his oversight, *he* had been the one to bring it up and even suggested a remedy. The boss jumped on the mistake to batter Doug by imputing to him a malevolent motive, which was not his in any way, and by doing so publicly. If Doug had been seeing more clearly he would have acknowledged his error but doggedly resisted the outlandish charge that he had a hostile motive. In the meeting, he would have said, "You're right about my mistake. Fire me if you want, but you're totally wrong about why I made it." If the boss persisted, Doug would have said, "You're not being fair."

As for the boss's use of a public forum, it would have been wrong for Doug to oppose that in public; then he would have been using the forum himself. However, he could have spoken to the boss later in private, saying something like, "If I make a mistake, I'll admit it. But it really makes it harder for me to do a good job if people go to meetings and hear you say that I'm a jerk."

Always ask yourself, "How much of the accusation against me is true?" Beware of people who tell you what your motives were. In general, people have no right to do this. And they certainly have no right to use speculations about your inner life as a pretext for assaulting you. Oppose them when they do, or they will form a Projection of you as contemptible, transparent, and insignificant.

Also, you never to have sit still for any inappropriate show of force against you: bitter sarcasm, shouting, public humiliation, any act of demotion or withdrawal of privilege that you think is unwarranted. No position or rank entitles others to treat you that way, and loyalty to yourself requires that you tell people not to, in no uncertain terms. Recall the advisability of being "oversensitive:" take exception quickly and don't hesitate to go to a higher authority for help or start looking for another job.

If the accusation is completely false, then of course you must rebut it without apology. Give evidence for its falseness. But try not to implicate others as your mode of escape.

Whether an accusation is true, false, or partially true, above all, don't become defensive or start spewing forth excuses. When you show another person that you feel you must defend yourself to the death against his charge, you invite him to see you as *in his power.* You must either admit a mistake cleanly or admit *only* the part that is true, staunchly denying what is false. Or you must declare the whole accusation untrue. The issue is seldom the incident itself but the Projections that are set in motion by how you handle the accusation.

WHEN YOU'RE
THE BOSS

If you supervise other people, it's almost a sure bet that many of them misperceive you. If you went by their pictures of you, you'd be twelve different people. One person sees you as gullible, another as deadly, and a third as absolutely fair. Scrutiny might reveal that your actions have little or nothing to do with how these pictures were formed. Each employee holding an intransigent Projection of you may have seen his previous bosses as very much like you and will go on seeing very little difference in other bosses.

The employee with some Projection on you has started working for you with a lightly etched expectation of what you, as a "boss," *might* be like.

When he applied for a job in Margie's company, Ben gave as a work reference someone who was really a distant relative and had never employed him. In his interview, he told Margie how proud he would be to work for her real estate firm, adding that everyone in the industry spoke of her in glowing terms. Actually, Ben had never heard of Margie and, when he met her, didn't even know whether he liked her or not: he was too busy conning her. With his performance he began stamping in his view that Margie was gullible and a fool.

Soon after Margie hired Ben he began experimenting

with bigger lies—about how many people he had brought to see a particular apartment, and how he had gotten a customer to raise his offer when this wasn't so. Since Margie wasn't paranoid and gave her employees some latitude, Ben got away with his lies. Within a few months, he convinced himself that Margie was an idiot, and he starting taking money from customers under the table. As Ben's Projection of Margie's stupidity grew, his offenses became more flagrant. Fortunately Margie caught him before he did any real harm and fired him on the spot. Ben was wrong: Margie was no fool, just another in a succession of employers who had bounced him when he underestimated them.

Also working for Margie was Angela, a very religious and ethical woman whose career was her life. She was excellent at her job: real estate owners knew she would always be truthful with them, and customers trusted her at once. Angela dedicated herself to filling out every line of every form as if it were a matter of life and death. Her co-workers, especially Ben, kidded her about being too meticulous about details. She was the first to arrive each day and the last to leave.

Six years previously, in her job interview with Margie, Angela had admitted her inexperience in the business, but Margie had told her, "I like you. I'll give you a chance to prove yourself." The next day, however, Angela had felt pangs of fear and remorse. She called Margie and said, "Before you hire me, there's something I want to tell you. I had some trouble two years ago with a bank loan. I didn't pay it back in time. I wanted to be sure that wouldn't get in the way." Margie had said, "Don't let it worry you. Just be here next Monday."

But over the years, Angela *had* worried about that and everything else. And she had *acted* on these worries: they had ruled her life. She would often go in on Saturdays and recalculate her week's tallies to be sure there were no mis-

218 Dr. George Weinberg and Dianne Rowe

takes. When construction contractors or electricians sent her Christmas gifts such as liquor or even cheese baskets, she would rush to hand them over to Margie. Of course, Margie would always refuse them. No matter how Margie sought to reassure Angela of her status and security, Angela kept feeling that Margie still hadn't decided whether Angela had "proven" herself. By her own compulsive actions, her fearful belief that any forgotten detail could be her doom, Angela kept convincing herself that Margie was to be dreaded. When Ben was fired, she had no doubt that her time was coming soon.

Lynn, who was Angela's best friend in the firm, had a totally different picture of Margie. Lynn had worked in a number of real estate firms, for good and bad bosses. She had seen the whole gamut—sexism, chicanery, naïveté, alcoholism—in her employers. In her view, Margie was totally fair and a pleasure to work for. "Can't you see the difference between you and Ben?" Lynn asked Angela. "He was stealing right and left. If Margie hadn't caught him, we might *all* have lost our licenses!"

From the very beginning, Lynn had been straight with Margie, admitting failures and celebrating successes. Her evenness of performance reinforced her view of Margie as "fair and reasonable." In fact, once when Lynn felt short-changed on a deal, she went to Margie to ask for the money she felt she deserved—and got it. On another occasion, she admitted that she'd made a bad deal through poor negotiation. Margie winced but said, "Don't brood about it. We all make mistakes." All along Lynn did exactly what she felt was right, so she retained a very clear view of her boss.

Here we see three different pictures of the same person. The first two were Projections: Margie had done nothing to warrant Ben's view of her as a fool or Angela's view of her as a dangerous taskmaster. Of the three, only Lynn saw Margie realistically—a lucky break for Margie, since she could feel relaxed with Lynn and rely on her for advice and understanding.

As with nearly all Projections, these two on Margie had a long history.

Ben had grown up playing his divorced parents against each other. He had discovered the advantages of lying to one parent about privileges granted by the other: "Mommy always lets me stay up until midnight on weekends." He would let a parent fear loss of status with him in order to get what he wanted: "Well, if *you* won't buy me a new bicycle, then Daddy will." He saw the benefits of laying it on thick in his praise of whichever parent he was with at the time. All of this reaffirmed his belief that his parents were indeed gullible. It was quite natural for Ben to carry this belief and the behavior sustaining it with him into the job world. He would soon convince himself by his treacherous actions that every authority could be fooled in the same way his parents were.

Angela's parents *were* dangerous taskmasters. They never hit her, but they would stop talking to her and curtail her activities for days if she failed to do her chores or if her grades were under par. They went berserk if she told anything less than the whole truth, and they sent her to a very stringent all-girls' school. Angela married a man that her parents virtually chose for her. He was much older than she was and very demanding. It was when he died that she went to work for Margie.

She was ready to see Margie as a punitive disciplinarian and dealt with her accordingly. Her whole methodology with Margie, designed to stave off disaster, projected on Margie an identity that was a combination of "mother" and "rigorous headmistress."

Because people will go on creating their own Projections of you, often by acts of theirs that you don't even see, don't expect to be universally loved by those who work for you.

AXIOM XLV: As a boss, you will be up against a variety of views of you, many of which are partly or completely Projections. You may be unable to stem them. Expect them and don't blame yourself.

The real issue is whether the person is doing the job, which may include not undermining you or others.

The main thing you can do is to act fairly and with dignity. People projecting may wrongly accuse you of mistreating them. If it's a real Projection, the person is likely to attribute to you not just misdeeds but *motives* that his parents had or seemed to have.

If you suspect that a Projection is at work, check it out by speaking with the employee privately. Question the person directly about the attitude of his that seems misguided. Let the person say his piece without interrupting in any way. Then, question the person about conclusions he's drawn, considering the evidence as dispassionately as you can. Here's a sample dialogue:

Henry calls Deborah in to talk. "You seem to be very unhappy with me. What's going on?"

Deborah says, "You never liked me here, not from the first day."

Henry asks, "What makes you think so?"

"A hundred things," Deborah says. "First of all, you favor the men, you give them the good assignments. They dote on you. You have an 'old boy' network."

"Go on."

"Well, I'm much better on the phone than Phil. Yet you chose him to call the big Cleveland account, not me. And why should I get less money than Frank? Experience isn't everything. And at the conference when you thanked people, I was last, and you didn't sound very enthusiastic. And that comment you made when I asked for more money—

'Prove yourself'—Why should I have to prove myself? Did Phil prove himself? . . .''

A flurry of answers occur to Henry; so many so fast that he's hard put to let Deborah finish. Rejoinders flood his mind, one after another, which might utterly crush Deborah if he put them into words: "You're not better than Phil, and Frank has a much better track record. Underpaid? Why after all that whispering against me at meetings, I would have fired you a long time ago if it weren't for the union and for some misplaced compassion I have for you.''

But Henry's first responsibility as boss is to reduce tension and keep the work environment peaceful. He might best do this by offering, at this point, as much reassurance as he comfortably can: "Look, Deborah, I'm glad you finally came in and told me what you've been feeling. You haven't done yourself any harm in talking to me. You've cleared the air, since we've both felt the stress for some time. But you're absolutely wrong about my motives.''

Henry, if he is totally innocent, is almost certainly disgusted at Deborah's accusations and competitive whining. A diatribe like hers would provoke the worst impulses in anyone.

But as part of his effort to restrain himself and to be fair, it would help if Henry asked himself *exactly what feelings* Deborah induces in him. Anger and a profound feeling of being misunderstood, obviously. (Note that if Henry were Deborah's therapist, he would study her misperceptions in great detail, reviewing her childhood with her and helping her to see exactly how she affects other people and why she distorts as she does. Perhaps Deborah had to cope with sexist parents who downgraded her alongside her brothers. Or perhaps Deborah's parents were abusive and irrational toward *all* their kids.)

But obviously, Henry isn't Deborah's therapist. He

should only be concerned with her job performance, including her effect on the morale of others. His goal in identifying the feelings Deborah induces in him must be to determine whether Deborah holds a Projection and, if so, what it is.

In scrutinizing his reactions, Henry realizes that he feels guilty and accused by Deborah's words, though he *knows* he has been treating her fairly. In fact, he has been almost deferential with her because of her complaining nature. Henry is angered, as well, at having overextended himself to please her when he might not have done so for more deserving employees. He recognizes that when he is around Deborah he has a gnawing desire to acquit himself, as if to still her accusations, and he feels burdened by her. He realizes that she *is* projecting; he has not mistreated her in any way.

From his analysis of his reactions, and the recognition that he has already been behaving toward Deborah with undue trepidation and an exaggerated fear of displeasing her, he can also infer that Deborah's Projection is hostile. Deborah sees him as someone who is against her and who is deliberately shortchanging her at every turn.

To whatever extent you, as boss, can puncture any Projection, it must be in the usual way: by getting the person to start *acting* differently towards you.

Henry should *not* try to get Deborah to change her mind at this stage. He should, instead, focus only on getting her to change her behavior. This will have the twofold effect of inducing Deborah to see him differently and, even before she does, of getting her to do a better job.

He might say, for instance, "Please, be careful not to bad-mouth me at meetings or ever to tell a client that I'm difficult. That doesn't help you with the client or with me, or me with the client. If you work positively, I'm sure all this can be ironed out. I won't bear any grudges and I don't want you to either."

The meeting might end with a handshake, and be followed up by a few special displays of interest on Henry's part.

AXIOM XLVI: To whatever extent your assault on an employee's Projection succeeds, it will do so only if you prevail on the person to act differently toward you.

Observe that the whole process of getting an employee to halt a Projection of you follows the outline given for changing *anyone's* Projection of you. But of course, the difference is that if you *fail* to thoroughly change an employee's erroneous picture of you, it matters less than with a lover or a close friend. The important thing is that you get the person to do his job.

SUMMARY

Whether you are primarily an employee or a boss, much of your success in business depends on how *you* view your job and how *others* view you.

With what you now know about the Projection Principle, you can exert much more control over your fate in the office than you might have imagined—over how you feel about going to work each day, and over how you are treated while you are there.

Keeping up your own healthy Projections on your boss, employees, and co-workers is essentially a matter of staying honest and not letting fear motivate you and convince that your job is undesirable. It may be hard but you will have the best career success, you will foster the best Projections *on* yourself, and the best Projections *for* yourself on others, if you force yourself to act with your business associates as if you don't need them for survival.

If you're repeatedly underestimated or misjudged in the office, it's not simply "bad luck." People grapple in subtle ways to establish a hierarchy, and small actions of yours will determine whether you gain or lose status.

Be aware of the good and bad Projections that may result when you make demands, give or take advice, complain, interrupt or accept interruptions, give or take compliments, and make accusations.

If *you* are a boss, it's almost certain that those under you will form Projections of you. Many of these will be based on their own parental models. Your employees may see you, for instance, as fair or unfair, tolerant or intolerant, soft or hard.

Realize that you may not have the time or the leverage to correct all such Projections. Expect them and don't blame yourself. What matters is whether the person is doing the job, and whether he is undermining you or others. To the extent that you *can* deal with a Projection, as always, it must be by prevailing upon the person to *act* differently towards you.

11

ROMANTIC LOVE

No perception adorns another person more than love. To be in love is to overlook faults or not care about them; it is to assign very different standards to ourselves and the one we love. Lovers may endure mistreatment from a newcomer in their lives that they would not accept from friends of long standing. Love has many kinds of insecurity in it: We worry about whether the other person loves us, about our adequacy, about the other person's happiness and perhaps his physical health. Our own concerns may seem less important. The money that we had intended to save we plunge into one unforgettable Christmas present. Love in all its forms is the discovery of self through the loss of self.

Romantic love is a very special kind of love. Indeed, attempts by certain psychologists to explain it in an entirely rational way look insane, fatuous—the attempts themselves almost seem to suggest that those psychologists have never been in love. It's as is a person set out to use words, pure words, to conjure up the experience of a color.

The very essence of love is its spontaneity. It appears in unlikely places, between people of very different ages, different races, different social strata; between people of the same sex and people of opposite sexes. If a whimsical deity were to contrive a rebellious impulse, one refusing to bend to the orthodox dictates of society, an impulse refusing to comply even with common sense, it would be romantic love. It is both delicate and powerful, like the tender flower that grows up through the cracks in the city sidewalk.

Romantic love develops privately. We can fall in love from afar or in a situation in which, close as we are, the other person does not know how we feel. Moreover, love's combustible matter is not the stuff that makes civilization go forward smoothly. We quit a business deal with a person who's late or dishonest, but love may actually thrive on such affronts.

Only the most stunted among us could deny the worth of this experience. And only the most rational and enervated among us can deny its irrational element or confuse romantic love with friendship. Heine and Voltaire wrote that friendship begins where love ends, and Santayana took pains to distinguish between those in our coterie of friends and those in our "pantheon"—the ones we love romantically.

There is another kind of love, which we might call "existential love." It is love based on the recognition of our frailty as fellow mortals, abandoned on this earth, responsible for our decisions as individuals; it is love based on the universal truth that we are going to die. Saint-Exupéry had this sentiment in mind when he wrote that love is "not two people looking into each other's eyes, but two people looking in the same direction." We may feel such love for our children, our parents, our siblings, perhaps our dear friends, for some fellow workers and people whose lives we comprehend emotionally—even for others we may not know but whose struggle on earth we admire. But it is very different from romantic love.

We've all used variations of the idea that a thing is "lovingly" done when referring to craftsmanship, to art, to human sacrifice of any kind, even to drudgery. We think of love as a requisite to performance of the highest order of excellence. Fame itself seems empty without the idea of sharing it or feeling loved.

Goethe said that "a few sips from the cup of love are what make all the struggle on this earth worth while." Probably most of us would agree.

On the other hand, nearly all therapists have had highly capable people come into their offices deeply in love and desperately unhappy. These people condemn themselves for sacrificing to the utmost for someone who they know does not love them in return. Though they are able to discern what's going on, even to the point of describing it to the therapist as unfair or ridiculous or hopeless, they just can't stop themselves. Artists who've dedicated themselves to their careers may cease working when a love affair is going wrong. Professional men and women tell therapists frankly that they never cared about their life's work one-tenth as much as they cherish the one person they love, who they know is mistreating them. They may recognize as well as the therapist does that they can never win the person over by prostrating themselves, that they are only making things worse; yet they insist on trying, going ahead in their desperately wrong direction. The alternative—quitting, giving up—seems too awful, too terrible to contemplate.

PROJECTION AND THE INTRAPSYCHIC PROCESS

The Projection Principle, though it cannot account for *why* we love a particular person, can show us how to sustain love when it is good for us and how to fall out of love when it's hurtful. The Projection Principle can help us to correct imbalances and revive love when it falters. Most of all, it can tell us how to nurture love and keep it from withering. Think of love as a delicate being whose life has been entrusted to you. The mystery of this life is beyond you, but you retain the power to enhance it or, if you're careless, to destroy it. The choices we make that influence our impression of the other person are decisive.

Most of us give a lot of thought to how our behavior is going to affect our lover, both in the courtship stage of a relationship and, it is to be hoped, afterwards. The plethora of books on doing better in relationships has sensitized us more than ever to what the other person needs. "Couple counseling" has become very popular. But therapists tend to see every love relationship as an exchange and too often settle for simply trying to find out what each of the partners really wants and letting the other person know what it is.

However, this kind of oversimplification assumes that love is really a kind of deal—"You give me what I want, and I'll do the same for you." Such an analysis is so far off the mark as to be preposterous. Psychologists, who are quite often too reductionistic, seem to be at their worst when talking about love. The plain truth is that we often love people who don't give us what we want and fail to love people who do.

An understanding of Projections is necessary to understand why some love affairs flourish and others die, why some people are easily able to fall in love while others can't.

The way partners *act* toward each other in a relationship affects not only the other person; it constantly affects each partner's own private picture of the other and of the relationship. To talk simply about a trade based on a "market analysis" of those involved is to miss this point. Love exists in people's *minds;* it's not something one can simply purchase. For instance, as we mentioned earlier, when you lie to someone you may make him seem stupid to you, even if he isn't. If you keep reminding your mate to do something you may convince yourself that he's forgetful or lazy or that he doesn't give a damn about you. Most extramarital affairs, even if the person doesn't get caught, dim that person's ability to see beauty and value in his mate.

In short, the impact of your actions on relationships is not just *interpersonal*—between you and your mate; it is *intrapsychic*—some of the effects of what you do take place *entirely within you.* By your actions, you are sending messages to your own mind about your partner. You may be convincing yourself that the other person is worthless or dangerous or boring or bored with *you.*

Spotting the behavior that is propagandizing you against a person you once loved is crucial if you are to understand what's happening in your relationship.

Moira could see that she was falling out of love with Brad. Nothing about him seemed to have the luster it had two years ago, when she'd met him. Now she was having second thoughts about marrying him. But everyone in Moira's life liked Brad better than ever, and they couldn't understand what was wrong with Moira.

"You're *always* disillusioned," her best friend Audrey told her angrily. "Why don't you give the guy a chance before you start thinking about breaking it up?"

Audrey and some others took Moira out to dinner and

virtually called her a spoiled brat. They praised Brad for his generosity, his honesty, and his sensitivity to Moira's needs. They told Moira that it was *she* who had changed, not Brad. Audrey reminded Moira of how hard she had worked to win Brad's love at the start of the relationship: "Don't you remember how excited you were, and how you used to love hearing Brad's opinions? Look at yourself. Now all you do is expect him to put up with your tantrums and your neglect!"

Realizing how much her friends cared for her, Moira decided to heed their advice and examine her *own* behavior to see what she might be doing that made Brad suddenly look so unappealing to her.

Moira saw it was true that those "tantrums" Audrey had talked about were indulgences that she wouldn't have permitted herself when she'd first met Brad. In those days, when she was trying to get him to fall in love with her, she had accepted him as he was and enjoyed him. Now she picked at him about everything: his laugh, his choice of tie, his job, even his opinion of a movie they'd seen. If he tried to defend himself at all against her whining, she'd get furious. She'd blow up if he ever asked to change some plans they had made.

And Moira realized something even worse. After an evening together, if Brad protested that she'd been unfair to him, Moira would instantly cut him off. She no longer cared to listen to Brad's thoughts or to consider that he might be hurt. In the past, hearing him out would have been a matter of life and death. Even if she had an early meeting the next day and felt shaken by what he was telling her, Moira used to insist that Brad go on speaking until he had voiced all his concerns. Though she was tearful at the time, she would feel better afterwards, closer to him, and glad that the two of them had cleared the air.

Moira's readiness to hear what Brad had to say, to sit up

with him until she was sure things were all right, even when she was tired or anxious about the next day, had reaffirmed in Moira's own mind her love for Brad. Such choices had helped her project on him, "the man I would do anything for, the most important person in my life."

Subsequently, her decision *not* to do this, to conserve her strength for other things, reduced Brad to just another of Moira's "activities." Furthermore, it caused her to see Brad's protests as excessive and out-of-place. Without his knowing it, Brad was becoming a burdensome character in Moira's eyes. By avoiding confrontations and curtailing her investment in him, Moira was convincing herself, "Brad is not the man for me."

But Brad really *was* the man that Moira wanted and the fine person that Moira's friends perceived him as being all along. Conceivably he might have salvaged his reputation with Moira by confronting her earlier and more firmly and by pointing out how she was cutting corners with him. But Brad, who was generous and untutored in such matters, allowed Moira her "moods" and gave her enough rope to strangle *him.*

Fortunately the decisive action of Moira's friends made her see what she was doing and she changed in time to revive the love affair.

In this case Moira's friends could see the interpersonal problems between her and Brad: It was obvious that she was unfair to him, that she didn't listen to him. However, only instinct told them that the real problem was occurring in Moira's own mind, that she was *causing herself to fall out of love by an intrapsychic process.* Luckily, the very actions they got her to reconsider were the ones that were destroying Moira's ability to love Brad.

Even amid a sea of interpersonal turmoil, intrapsychic effects keep piling up in the minds of the participants. Lovers are constantly adding new touches to their picture of each other. When a love relationship seems successful, it is not because it is frozen into a "stable" form. Rather, every relationship is a living organism that requires steady acts of nourishment.

And when things go wrong between people you can be sure that, long before there are visible flare-ups, each partner has been incubating a harmful Projection of the other. Intrapsychic effects caused by the way the people *treated* each other gave rise to the interpersonal clash. The overt trouble between partners when it erupts is nearly always a late development. This is why it is so important for therapists not to overemphasize the surface battles between partners at the expense of their underlying Projections.

ROMANTIC
PROJECTIONS
—

All love is idealism. Love is sustained by giving more than is required, by those very investments in the other person and in life that hard reality doesn't demand of us. The real creations, the things that set humans apart from other animals, from brutes are, by necessity, forms of excess—*romantic Projections,* if you prefer.

AXIOM XLVII: Romantic love, when it is genuine and returned, is the only form of Projection that you might *never* want to change. It can coexist with reality: in fact, it colors the reality, transfiguring daily events into lofty experiences.

It is not enough to describe love as Freud did, as "an impulse with an inhibited aim," obliquely calling it a form of stunted sexual expression. Or to ignore or disrespect it as the behaviorists have done, or to call it a neurosis.

Romantic Projections, those curious forms of excess, are what give life its special meaning. It is precisely the amount extra, beyond what is required, that engenders love and keeps it alive over time.

Though we cannot define love, we can pinpoint the acts that sustain it. No one is too insignificant to love or to maintain a love relationship, and no one is deprived of the means, since the acts that create love derive their value not from their size but from their intention. What all such acts have in common is that they reach beyond what is necessary or expected of us.

Of course, there can be no doubting the danger of romantic Projections. Some argue that such Projections are distortions, denials of reality, and that the cost is so great when the bubble bursts that we are well-advised not to form such grandiose pictures in our minds.

Such romantic Projections may indeed become obsessions. Often the person subject to them doesn't even enjoy sex with his lover—he's too anxious about his performance and it's hard to connect with someone who's more ideal than real. It's wonderful to be someone else's dream-come-true and even better to be so in love that reality hardly matters, but it had better be with the right person.

And yet romantic Projections can and do *coexist* with reality. After all, what beauty would we see if we thought of its value only in terms of hard facts? Think of the skull beneath the skin and beauty is gone, think of time's fell hand, of waste and decay, think of all pursuits as ultimately hopeless and it becomes a defensible to say that nothing we do would matter were it not for romance. A tincture of romantic Projection seems necessary to make all love and friendship worthwhile.

The form of idealism that coexists with reality is the one

that allows us to love people more instead of less as they age, that never disdains frailty. We sustain this idealism by never laughing at weakness or joining society when it condemns the victim. Such a romantic view, which in the poet Percy Shelley's words bewails "the frailty of all things here," is the very basis for love. We would do well to select acts that keep this romantic view alive and to shun acts that weaken it.

Psychology, with its insistent reductionism, has been at its worst when it has sought to explain love or even friendship scientifically, ignoring the magic that sustains relationships and makes them special.

PREPARING
FOR ROMANTIC LOVE
―

From earliest childhood, you've been making choices and sifting influences in your own personal way, gradually forming an image of your own "ideal lover." As in a fairy tale that is retold over centuries the details may evolve but, for most of us, the essence changes surprisingly little.

The familiar has fleshed out your "ideal." You've admired certain people—a parent, a family friend. You may have "fallen in love" with a movie actor or actress or with a high romantic character in a book. But the soul of your ideal is grafted from your own. The person you dream of embodies certain strivings of yours.

Sophie wanted to be a great pianist and, by time she was twelve, she had a large record collection and was saving all her money to go to concerts. She was very popular in school, and had a lot of friends. But she always preferred the company of an older person who had just come back from a concert in town.

Sophie was very talented at math, but to her it was merely an exercise, unadorned by a dream. She preferred reading about nineteenth-century music, which few others in her circle cared about. Her great-uncle, Max, who was a piano teacher in Chicago, and her image of Franz Liszt, whom she felt she knew well from his photographs in a book Max gave her, fused into Sophie's romantic ideal. In high school, her music teacher's son, who taught her some harmony and counterpoint, was added to the pastiche.

Sophie was very pretty and was always in demand. But the few boys that she actually went out with seemed to her boring and immature. She dreamed of finding a man talented, lonely, misunderstood, a genius at music who would love her. It mattered little to her if he was older and distinguished like Uncle Max, or young and spectacular like Liszt himself.

To a casual observer, it might seem that this burning image of lover-hero spurred Sophie's emphasis on music. This was certainly so. However, a more important truth is that Sophie's devotion to music emblazoned in her mind the picture of the man she wanted.

Sophie's struggle against adults and peers who told her that classical music promised no future, who wanted her to "be a kid" and have more of a social life, who felt she was "odd" or "old-fashioned," made music and its heroes all the more important to her. Her long hours of practice, her obsession with working through any faults in her technique, the determination that made her travel a whole afternoon to hear an evening concert in another town, her spending days searching through catalogues for a rare record or piece of sheet music—all this made it seem unthinkable that she could ever love a man who was not musical.

In college Sophie fell in love with an assistant professor who taught conducting. He was highly competitive with her, and the relationship did not go well. Sophie was graduated with honors and went to New York with a scholarship to Julliard. During her studies at Julliard and later, when she began getting some promising concert bookings, Sophie continued to look for a man in the mold of those she dreamed about.

Unable to make a go of it with the various men in the music profession whom she dated, Sophie took a chance on a relationship with Victor, a stock market analyst whom she met at a benefit for music students.

Although Victor had absolutely no musical talent of his own, he loved the idea of music and sought it as refuge from his own workplace turmoil. Sophie saw in him the sensitivity, loneliness, and *romanticism* that she had hoped to find in a performer. And there was a side of him that Sophie had unconsciously sought, something that was missing in herself. Victor brought balance, common sense, worldliness, and a robust understanding of how people interacted, which Sophie knew she lacked. Victor was a variation on the lover-hero theme that Sophie had always played in her mind.

As with your career or anything you've dreamt about, the lover you choose is usually an evolved version of your earliest picture.

AXIOM XLVIII: By striving in some direction and eliminating other directions, by deciding what you value and investing in it, you identify the kind of person you will some day love. That person will embody qualities that you yourself have made important.

The second feature of the lover you choose is that the person *imports* into your life qualities that you want and do not possess. This theory of import, espoused by the psychologist C. A. Tripp, says that we tend not to duplicate what we have already. Sophie had the musical talent and Victor appreciated it; Victor, on the hand, had the hard-nosed ability to grapple with people that Sophie admired but could not muster herself.

AXIOM IL: Just as the artist creates for himself what's missing in his own life, we seek to import, through a lover, what's missing in our lives and in ourselves.

The ways in which your efforts in some direction can crystalize your image of the lover you're looking for are infinitely various. Great concern over your appearance or excessive involvement with diet and exercise may shine the spotlight on physical attractiveness or youth in a lover. Your desire for social prestige may impel you toward powerful men or women, *not* only to share in their power but because they embody everything you care about. It might be a drive toward the unconventional or a dread of being controlled by people that has motivated you over the years; if so it will endear to you revolutionaries, radicals, outcasts of any kind.

Your ideal lover may evolve out of your all-consuming passion and lifetime preferences, as with Sophie. But the more usual case is that the person is a combination of much that you care about, taking hints of color from qualities that you've striven for. He is more of a composite and less of an idée fixe.

Most of this works unconsciously. This is especially true of your "imports." Maybe you lack forcefulness and are unconsciously drawn to it in other people. You might gravitate toward delicacy or even fragility if toughness has been a way of life for you.

Perhaps one of the most widespread sexual turn-ons since

the world began is a hint of coarseness. The fast-talking prostitute in movies, the mercenary-soldier image, the lover who verges on brutality—these people offer a quality that many are afraid of in themselves but desire in a sexual lover. As the authors of genre romances know, it's hard to feel wanted if the other person maintains his gentility to the end.

Traits that convention demands we subdue in ourselves often emerge as virtues we desire in a lover. If we've been told in youth to keep our thoughts to ourselves, we're attracted toward people who express theirs openly. And we're nearly all attracted to a sense of humor in a lover because of the enormous release it affords and the openness it implies.

AXIOM L: Both our strivings and what we lack influence our picture of our ideal lover and predispose us to a certain kind of romantic Projection.

PACING
YOURSELF

Some people project on a love relationship the image of a sixty-yard dash while others see it as a marathon. The sprinters try to take what they can quickly, knowing the race will soon be over. They often encourage their lover to do too much for them—to spend too much money on them or devote too much time to taking care of them. They may ask a new lover almost nothing about himself, show no interest in him once they "have" him, and yet be bottomless in expressing their own needs.

Those with the marathon Projection don't necessarily talk about the future or try to ensnare lovers into lifetime obligations. Rather, they relate to the person in depth as though there were limitless time. When the lover or would-be lover offers more than he can afford to give, the marathon person discourages him, perhaps refusing outright to take so much. If in conversation the lover quickly passes over the difficulties of his life, the marathon person, who really cares, will slow him down and communicate a concerned attitude—not as a device to ingratiate herself but because a relationship is best when there is mutuality, even a relationship that turns out to be short-lived for other reasons.

The marathon person, who is capable of building lasting relationships, may have the sensitivity not to let a lover exalt him if it means putting himself down. He might conceivably interrupt and disagree when a distortion—even one that inflates him—is in progress. This is important because many Projections have a backlash: the person gives too much and then can't keep it up or decides you're not worth it and ultimately resents you. Ideally, the other person should run only as fast as he can while breathing comfortably, and you should do the same.

Part of pacing is remembering that every single act of yours affects your view of your lover and the relationship. You must learn to anticipate the Projective effects of your acts, both large and small, even ones that the other person knows nothing about.

For example, you may choose to confide a fact in your mate, even though you expect it will make him angry. You do this because you don't want to assign to him the part of hopeless curmudgeon and make yourself afraid of him. You take the time to work around the house, even though it's your lover's home, because you want to feel that when you're there, it's *your* home, too. You explain something complex about your work because you want to see your lover as capable of learning about it. You do many things partly because you want to feel that the person will be in your future and not just in your present. Though you might make such decisions automatically, when in doubt, you can best predict their likely consequences by using the Projection Principle.

HOW
LOVE DIES

Love, like life, can end in countless ways: wordlessly, as when a traveler freezes in the silent North, or in hot dispute; through stinginess or by being frittered away. And love dies alone in every breast, just as life ends alone, whether we're a thousand miles from help or surrounded by attendants. Even after we're told one morning that the other person doesn't love us and has found somebody else, our own love has many stages to undergo before it dies. The death of our own love, still to come, may be more painful than the recognition that the other person no longer loves us. It feels to us like the death of love in the universe.

Of course, as we now know, love doesn't die of its own accord; someone kills it, maybe *both* partners simultaneously. Let's look at the four chief murder weapons.

DEATH BY STARVATION:
THE LAW OF ECONOMY

Perhaps the most common household killer of love is the one we've already studied: the law of economy. A lover who feels secure does less for his loved one, dispensing first with those very necessary "excesses" and gradually omitting even some common courtesies. Not realizing that he is doing it, he deprives the other person of what made her special in the first place.

We have seen that romantic love is built on excesses: by nature it is transcendent, beginning when ordinary interchange can go no further. Its very magic and fragility demand that it be treated with the utmost care.

The law of economy is lethal to romantic love because romantic love thrives on extravagance.

Geoffrey, who is trying to win his beloved, Nora, associates a hundred ordinary daily experiences with her. He has her in mind when he buys a certain necktie or stays in the gym twenty minutes longer. He connects her with a character in a novel he's reading and compares other women unfavorably with her in his mind; he searches for the out-of-print book she mentioned casually and buys tickets four months in advance for a play she might like.

If anyone were to tell Geoffrey, "You think about Nora too much," he'd wouldn't even understand what the person meant. And almost nothing in practice seems too much to do for her.

Obviously these giddy heights are impossible to sustain as a relationship progresses. Suppose Geoffrey wins Nora and marries her. The future of their romantic love both reflects and depends upon the degree to which he resists economizing—dropping the excesses without replacing them.

If their love affair is to continue for a lifetime, it is true that more practical elements must enter. Maybe they can't afford to see every play Nora would like. But now, instead of always looking out for advance theatre tickets, Geoffrey checks the local video rental store twice a week for movies they can see together. He's back on his regular gym schedule, and sometimes he buys a wild tie that he knows Nora won't like, but he's secretly putting money away to buy Nora the diamond engagement ring she always wanted for their fifth anniversary. He doesn't think about Nora all day long, and now he knows he can disagree with her without risking their relationship, but he still calls home to see how she's feeling if they've had an argument the night before, and he loves telling friends in the office about her new business venture.

By substituting new "excesses," Geoffrey has sustained the romantic love he always had for Nora.

If Geoffrey had succumbed to the law of economy, say because he felt he "had" Nora and didn't have to try anymore, or because he got "too busy" at work or with his hobbies, he might have hastened a decline in his romantic picture of her. Each default would have successively whittled away her image, making other economies easier. Instead of replacing theater tickets with video rentals, he might have left Nora to find her own "entertainment." Instead of calling her after a fight, he might have let her "get over it." Instead of praising her to friends and thinking he was lucky to have her, he might have begun seeing other women as preferable. Geoffrey might have "acted" himself out of love with Nora.

Almost anything can become a pretext for cutting corners with another person. Your mate turns out to have a bad temper or is slow getting ready in the morning or is forgetful. You take the easy way out by giving less and expecting less. But the real romantic lover makes capital even of these "deficiencies" since they afford the chance to give "excessively" by overlooking faults and loving the other person in spite of or even because of them.

BETRAYAL AS A MODE
OF DESTRUCTION

———

Betrayal, to nearly all of us, means sexual infidelity; how-ever, it may happen in myriad other ways.

For instance, Andy and Celia agree that Celia will support them both for three years while Andy finishes his doctorate. However, when his thesis is returned for major revisions, he decides not to pursue it but doesn't tell Celia. She goes on nurturing his dream of becoming a psychologist, which he knows will never happen. He allows the deception to go on for over a year.

Then it comes out. Finding that she just can't turn herself over to him as she did, that she can't make those same sacrifices, Celia is heartbroken. During the next year she falls out of love with him, and a year after that she leaves him. His betrayal hurt her, but what was worse, it made her feel foolish for doing the things she once did, which had affirmed her love for Andy and renewed it every day.

Even with sexual infidelity, which to the vast majority of us is the ultimate betrayal, it's not just the act but what it symbolizes; it usually entails a spiral of dishonesty. The person having the affair contrives to dupe his partner, to lie and cover up—all of which dampen his ardor and down-grade his partner's worth in his own mind. It is not the affair itself but the many dishonesties incident to it that ultimately sabotage his love. Moreover, it becomes hard for him to express love as he did formerly. Often while having the affair the person dispenses with acts of love toward his mate, or attempts to assuage his guilt by doing too much. Such atonement, which stems from fear, conflicts with love and reduces it further. Because the mind tends to simplify, betrayals provide their own arguments; they furnish their own excuses for being.

As for the victim, she may sustain her loving projection on an unfaithful mate. Ingenuously, she may keep on loving him, perhaps even blaming herself for the disaffection she senses in her husband. She's gotten too old or too fat—some limitation in herself that she always knew about has caught up with her. Not till she herself changes her behavior, perhaps in reaction to some inkling of having been betrayed, does her love also undergo decline.

Ironically, even imagined betrayal can be destructive to love. The person who suspects his partner of infidelity may embark on a pattern of behavior that suppresses love. Sensing betrayal, he projects a whole new image onto his mate. Such acts as questioning the other person, maintaining surveillance on her, stifling her freedom, accusing her outright—tests in any form—make the other person seem diabolical. All tests of other people foster Projections: it doesn't matter what you find; your testing itself imbues the person with the guilt you suspect. Perhaps going through her mail this one time has revealed nothing, but by so doing, you've convinced yourself just a little more that you had better keep watch. Even at best, love often entails some fear of loss; allowing yourself to act in accordance with that fear will magnify it and destroy love as fast as if you were betrayed.

MURDER
BY POLARIZATION
—

Polarization takes the adage "From each according to his means" to a ridiculous and destructive extreme. It typecasts the two people in a relationship as opposites of each other and implies that they can never switch roles.

Typically the parts the two play develop out of real differences between them—the person who is physically stronger does most of the heavy work around the house; the one more capable socially is likely to make the phone calls and write the thank-you notes for both; upon the partner who can fix things devolve most or all of the challenges when something in the house breaks down. But polarization *exaggerates* these differences in the minds of the partners to the point where they become caricatures, as if each is absolutely unable to operate in the other's sphere.

The physically stronger person is now seen as a "brute," or big and awkward; the weaker partner is seen as pathetically frail, unable even to carry a bag of groceries in from the car. The person more capable socially is seen as sophisticated, cosmopolitan, and the final judge on all matters of decorum while the other partner is depicted as bumbling, perhaps uneducated, a bit vulgar, and someone who would be lost without a guide. The household handyman assumes the proportions of a wilderness survival expert while the less talented partner, who sits and waits in the dark under burned out light bulbs, is seen, and sees herself, as hopelessly inept and unable to learn how anything works.

Often these role assignments mirror expectations. For instance, the woman shuns tasks requiring physical strength, even if she works out and can lift more weight than the man can. As a result, she projects onto the man the identity of being physically stronger than she is. Going even further, the man may be the more natural cook, but in keeping with his role as thick-fingered oaf he will assign kitchen chores to the woman, and she may willingly accept them in exchange for exemption from physical labor.

After a while, it becomes hard to separate real differences from role assignments that are nothing more than Projections. Nor would the partners necessarily *want* to separate the truth from fantasy. Polarization is a product of convenience, and each partner is served in the moment by having the other deal with unpleasant chores.

Furthermore, each person begins to *believe* his role in the home and to feel keenly the limits of his own identity. Once a role is accepted, the actor begins to add other behaviors consonant with this image, thus stamping in his erroneous view of his and his partner's contrasting identities.

It's as if each has become half a person—as if it takes the two of them to make a whole person, either partner alone being insufficient. There's an old Laurel and Hardy skit where the two of them appear at someone's home with pails of paint and brushes. The woman who greets them is surprised. "But we only advertised for one person," she says. To which Laurel replies deadpan, "Oh, we two can do the work of one, madam."

Polarization may actually add tang to a relationship, and to sexuality. Over the ages women have had to feign ignorance of sex; men were supposed to be the aggressors. The game of assuming these roles may appeal to both. But taken beyond the level of a game, polarization breeds Projections that have destroyed many love affairs. Who wants to spend a lifetime with a "brute" or a helpless, fading flower or a live-in Emily Post or a social incompetent or someone who sits in a dark room waiting for a light bulb to get changed? In the end the Projection fostered by the polarization, which the other person willingly accepts, kills romance.

For instance, Ed enjoyed his wife Jocelyn's energy in confronting people. He himself liked to play the saint, being gentle with everyone. He was fastidious, never raised his voice, and was so polite that it seemed as if he were constantly rebuking people for becoming distraught and making difficulties where there were none.

At a cocktail party or at a friend's house, on occasion Ed was attacked or questioned. He would simply smile while Jocelyn vehemently defended him: "How dare you imply that my husband was unfair to that gardener! You have some nerve."

Ed quietly enjoyed Jocelyn's defense of him and lived off her vitality, but in public he chastened her as if she were a child. While she was getting red-faced from defending his honor, Ed would criticize her with a statement like "Darling, you've made your point."

To others the two seemed mismatched—they were so different. However, apparent differences are often the reason such people choose one another. One partner wants someone who will give vent to impulses that he himself feels but is afraid to express. Ed chose Jocelyn for that very reason: because she readily expressed anger and manifested a personal force that he dared not experience in himself. In reality, he continually fed off her anger as it satisfied his own impulses. Insipid people who really have a lot of anger inside of them often choose mates who will express that anger for them.

Over time, Ed enjoyed the luxury of having Jocelyn clear up misunderstandings with airline stewardesses and bank tellers. When he bought an item that didn't seem to work, he would hand it to her to return to the store. She became a good fighter. "Darling," Ed would say softly, "you're better at bringing things back than I am." If it was a big item and she said, upon returning, "The store will let me know tomorrow," he would wince and let her know that she hadn't been tough enough. It was as if she were a pugilist and he were her coach.

It got to the point where, if their child vomited or the dog soiled the rug, Ed automatically left the room while Jocelyn cleaned up the mess.

Not a very romantic Projection in either direction, but such was their tacit understanding, and she was as responsible for the polarization as he was. She had steadily played into his expectation and made it her aim to satisfy his requirements.

However, things went downhill. At first Ed always let Jocelyn become the aggressor sexually; later he would delight in telling her that he was not in the mood. His sexual desire for her went down to almost nothing. His own non-romantic Projection onto her was the critical factor, though it's possible some natural lowering of drive over the years also played a part. But Ed couldn't acknowledge either: He was the eternal child. To himself, he blamed Jocelyn for not turning him on: "Her face has coarsened; her voice is harsh; she's too aggressive; I hate the way she walks; she's gaining weight."

Jocelyn soon surmised what she looked like to Ed and would often yell at him, though afterwards she would always try to make up. Ed, however, was unforgiving, and Jocelyn no longer had the interest to push the point. Next Ed began spending stretches of time away from her. But by then Jocelyn had allowed herself to see him as a wimp and a detractor and she wasn't sorry. She had fantasies of being with a "real" man. Then Ed started an affair with his secretary, who was much younger than Jocelyn. He was glad to make all the preparations for their stolen weekends on business trips. He overvalued the secretary's delicate features and her fondness for him.

To Jocelyn's delight, Ed finally left her. However, the secretary didn't see in Ed anything more than the chance to have a father figure dote on her. Ed had built a dream world out of his Projections. Almost too dainty for this world, he went to live by himself in a sterile high-rise but found that without Jocelyn around he had little to say to his teen-aged children.

When he asked Jocelyn if he could come back, she shouted at him, "I'm too coarse for you. I always was." She broke into tears; for the first time in many years he saw her as vulnerable and afraid and realized that he had always loved her. But Jocelyn never did take Ed back; she married another man, less successful in business than Ed, but more robust, and who saw her as she really was.

Polarization occurs to some degree in all relationships. It's the perceptual component of the division of labor. Certainly, there's nothing wrong with the appreciation of contrasts or with a healthy application of the saying, "From each according to his means."

But as Ed and Jocelyn proved, partners can use contrasts as weapons against each other in relationships. Ed used Jocelyn's ability to express honest indignation *against* her as the relationship went on. The more Jocelyn fought Ed's battles for him, the more she began to look like a loud-mouth hag to him. And the more Ed depended on Jocelyn, the more prissy and unmasculine he looked to her.

Any tendency toward systematically contrasting two people's talents in a relationship, if allowed to go haywire, may develop into a polarized Projection that can kill a romance.

MERGING AS A MURDER WEAPON

Merging is the chief way that lovers, despite their good intentions toward each other, may destroy love. A partner, through a succession of choices and actions, fuses with the other person in his mind, obliterating the lover as an individual and turning him into an extension of himself. The person who "merges" develops the Projection about the lover, "This person is me."

Usually merging evolves out of a natural desire to share. It is "togetherness" taken to a destructive extreme. In an effort to do things together, to understand each other, to communicate every trivial detail, to escape the inevitable isolation that life insists upon, the partners arrange as much of their lives together as they can. But what may look like an ideal love affair collapses as the two people become "of one mind." Each partner knows exactly what the other is going to do and think and feel; in fact, he will be doing the same himself. The mystery is gone.

What often happens is that each person sees in the other all of his own faults and limitations. Since the other person is "me," there is no surprise, no novelty, no romance. In the end, one partner feels the yearning for a real lover because one's present partner has been absorbed into the self.

Katherine was brought up to believe that marriage was very important—definitely meant to last forever. Her parents showed a united front at all times, never arguing around the children. Even when one parent was unjust to Katherine or one of her siblings, they could not take their case to a "higher court" by going to the other parent: Mom and Dad would never take sides against each other.

When she was seventeen, Katherine left home to enroll in a hotel management program in St. Louis; at nineteen she fell in love with Chris, a young man who was already a night manager where she worked. Chris was addicted to automobiles: fascinated by engines, design, special features, and everything connected with them. After the first few dates, when things started getting serious between them, Katherine decided that she should start to share Chris's interest. Soon she was reading his auto magazines and they would spend long hours working together on cars.

Eventually they married, and Katherine immediately arranged to have her work schedule changed so that she could be on the night shift with Chris. When Chris changed jobs and went to a hotel a few blocks away as day manager, Katherine went with him, taking a slight demotion. She wanted the most of Chris, and he felt the same way about her.

When their first child came, they were still living in a cramped studio apartment. Rather than take larger quarters, they opted for the adventure of being with each other in one room, while they saved toward a house.

They drove to and from work together, picked the baby up from the day-care center together, did the grocery shopping together, and tended to agree on most things. They told friends that it was wonderful to work in the same place because neither missed a thing in the other's day. From the outside, their marriage seemed ideal. Both blamed their seldom having sex any more on their incredibly busy schedule, what with the baby and their work. After all, their communication was excellent—they told each other almost everything they felt. They even joked about being "psychic" with each other. And when they learned to play bridge, each could practically decipher the other's hand from his facial expression. Their motto was that "everything can be worked out if only you talk about it."

But actually, without knowing it, they suppressed a lot of anger, and the truly taboo subject was boredom. Their Projection on the relationship evolved: "There's no one here but me."

After their second child was born, Katherine quit her job. She felt very depressed and attributed it to not seeing Chris all day. She also started having trouble controlling herself with Chris regarding something that had always been a sore point with her. Katherine, who was fanatical about dieting and staying slim, could hardly restrain great upset when Chris gained a few pounds or when he ate any of the rich foods that he loved. Now, it was *almost impossible* for her not to bark at him if he asked for a second helping, even when friends were around. It was as if he was stuffing food down *her* throat.

Then, with so much free time on her hands, Katherine fell to brooding about other things. Chris was not nearly as educated as she wanted him to be. He made mistakes in grammar. If he'd gotten a college degree he could go farther in the business and they'd both be better off. Katherine managed to suppress such thoughts for the sake of harmony in the marriage.

However, soon she found herself unable to perform the day's chores. After feeding the kids, she would discover that she'd been sitting in one place for an hour or two with an unopened magazine on her lap. She came to dread going out to do the shopping, and she begged off social engagements. Believing that the true cause of this malaise was that she missed Chris, she would call him at work and ask him to come home early, which he dutifully did. After a while, Chris was rushing home at all hours of the afternoon, dismayed to find Katherine moping and not doing her share. She began accusing Chris of infidelity, and when he didn't come to the phone immediately when paged, she said that people at the hotel were "covering up" for him.

In fact, Chris *did* have a brief affair with a woman he worked with at the hotel, someone very different from Katherine. The woman was a little older than Chris and highly independent, which made her seem "exotic" to him. But the affair ended abruptly when Katherine went into an acute depression; then Chris's life revolved around driving Katherine to her therapy sessions and finding reliable help to take care of the kids.

Fortunately the therapist was insightful, and she resisted Katherine's request that she see Chris too so that they might work on the "marriage" together. As the therapist had surmised, it turned out that Katherine's depression was the flip side of great rage toward her husband, which grew out of her merging with him over the five years they'd been a couple.

Katherine's Projection on Chris as "me" caused her to level at him every charge she would bring against *herself* had she been more honest emotionally. Her obsession with weight, her disappointment at her own lack of education and at not coming from a wealthy home to begin with— these things she blamed not on *herself* but on *Chris*. Having attributed all these familiar flaws to Chris, she could no longer see him as a lover. She hated to acknowledge that she yearned for someone else, someone from far away, someone less familiar, whose flaws, if any, would not be her own.

As for Chris, who had merged with Katherine in a similar way, he too was disillusioned with love and marriage so far as she was concerned. But instead of simply swallowing his despair, Chris had sought to banish it by losing himself in another relationship.

The therapist made the canny suggestion that Katherine begin coming to sessions on her own, without Chris driving her. Also, that it *was* permissible for her to have private ideas and feelings and not share them with Chris. This was not betrayal and would not weaken the marriage, but would strengthen it by reaffirming the individuality of the partners.

Katherine was able to alter her Projection on Chris as "me" and to see him as a romantic partner again. For Chris, the comeback was easier. He had more consciously resented the pressures of the merging, which he had levied on himself and Katherine had exerted on him. The time he spent at work, away from Katherine, gave him some healthy distance, and the two put their marriage back on course.

Sometimes it's hard to resist the articles and popular advice in favor of "togetherness" and "sharing" at all costs. But to prevent a relationship from foundering on the rocks of overexposure it's important to define yourself as different from the other person.

You are there by choice, not by inherent attachment. You have your own interests, tastes, preferences, and feelings. You are indivdually responsible for your choices, for your ethics, for your vision of life. True, we make sacrifices for one another, but any choice to do so must be our own. If you're sorry later, it's your responsibility to reconsider that choice and perhaps not make it again. Though other people can induce feelings in you, they cannot make you act.

Merging is the confusion of other people with yourself: It is the Projection onto other people that holds them accountable for what you do, and you accountable for what they do. It denies the inherent separateness of people and the obvious truth that we are each responsible for the consequences of our own decisions.

Merging typically leads the person to see his mate as his jailer—or in Jean-Paul Sartre's words, a living negation, as a "negative." Self-hatred turns into hatred of the other; self-doubts become distrust. Merging nearly always disposes us to form unwarranted Projections of the other person and introduces trouble in relationships, maybe not at first, but certainly after a while.

SUMMARY

These are, of course, only some of the Projections that occur in romantic relationships. Anyone can look back over his or her own involvements and, applying the Projection Principle, see his own performance and that of the other person in a new light.

Much happens in love affairs apart from how the people

affect each other as they interact. They are shaping their own vision all the while in ways that set the stage for love or make it impossible.

What is transcendent about love affairs that succeed is that your acts are more lofty than they have been before; in the process you teach yourself to see your lover as utterly different from anyone you have ever known.

12
CONCLUSION

Projections are all around you—people are projecting on you all the time.

It's normal and inevitable that others will add something of themselves to their vision of you, and in many cases that extra ingredient is in your favor. The tincture that another person adds to what is really there can turn attraction into love. Projections can turn a routine chore into a meaningful endeavour, and a friend into a golden ally.

As individuals, we project on our past and on our future. Even if as children we struggled and were often uncertain, we may remember mainly what was best about our childhood. Possibly we picture it as the happiest, most carefree time of our lives.

Our Projections grow with us. In college, we may have projected "obsolescence" on people over thirty-five. But now that we're past forty, we look back on our college years full of regret for wasted time and power. We think to ourselves, "I didn't know enough to get the most out of life back then." We project "confused beginner" on ourselves as a college student.

The key Projection we all hold about the past is that everything that happened was inevitable.

"I *had* to leave home; my parents were impossible."

"I *had* to finish college; it was obvious I'd get nowhere without it."

"I *had* to marry Glen; he was the only guy my parents liked."

Whether our decisions turned out for better or for worse, we tend to forget that there was choice involved. In our need for closure we erase the torment and conflict we suffered, substituting a Projection that our lives have moved in a steady straight line with everything falling into place naturally.

Regarding our Projection on the future, what's to come may seem "terrible" if we're currently depressed or lonely. Or it may seem "glorious" and "bright," if we've just started something big—a new job, a new relationship. Indeed, our Projections of the future are the very essence of our success. Our dream of ourselves at some time to come sustains us through drudgery now; it lights the way to all of our achievements.

Just as individuals project, so do whole cultures. Each generation has a slightly different view of past events. The people of the Middle Ages saw Classical culture as "dangerous" and "heathen," but those of the Renaissance saw the same ancient thinkers as part of a "Golden Age" to be valued and imitated. Similarly, those considered "rebels" in their own time may become "heroes" to a subsequent age, and not because any new knowledge is unearthed. Historical revisionists are simply seeing the past through the lens of their own culture.

And, of course, society's vision of the future is also a Projection, though it may vary from one country to another and from one decade to the next. From the flower-children's dream to the goals of a military-industrial complex, people's visions of the future shape their concept of progress and motivate their efforts. And from Thomas More's *Utopia* to Stanley Kubrick's movie *2001: A Space Odyssey,* creative artists have enjoyed conjuring up a picture of what will be.

However, as you've seen, Projections in our own daily lives can do us great harm. People who view you unfavorably and unfairly may treat you in ways that deprive you of money, opportunity, respect, or even love. Projections can cause you to be unacknowledged or unappreciated. The person you "just couldn't get through to" may have been insistently seeing you in the wrong light. For your own good, you must step in and attack Projections before they become so ingrained that you are powerless against them.

You have also seen that your own well-being, your capacity for happiness, depends on your recognizing your own Projections and controlling them. It is within your power to avoid the tragedy of failing to see love, opportunity, loyalty, and respect when they are there.

With what you now know, a wide range of everyday acts take on new meaning. You can see why certain things that people did, though they seemed small at the time, hurt you or upset you. You weren't just overreacting, as you thought. Things that seemed incomprehensible or unfair to you, such as someone's favoring the less deserving, now fall into place. You may also now understand how certain behaviors that always seemed objectionable really do damage relationships.

It is by actions, including those that seem insignificant, that people create and sustain Projections, and the key to changing Projections is to change actions.

Even when you aren't using the Projection Principle to improve a relationship, you can learn a great deal about the richness and variety of human nature by figuring out what people's Projections are.

It's interesting to play a game with yourself, asking, "What is this person's Projection?" Choose someone close to you to start with—your mate, a parent, a friend, a co-worker. Watch him in action. You may not uncover his Projection at once, but if you use the techniques you now have, you'll arrive at some fascinating conclusions:

"This guy who's always borrowing money from me thinks I'm his mother."

"Uncle Eliot thinks that just because the young secretaries in his law firm smile when he comes in, they're in love with him. He sees himself as 'irresistible' and them as 'pushovers.' "

"Genevieve thinks that her next-door neighbor will probably marry her if she keeps bringing him soup when he's sick and offering to do his shopping along with hers every week. She sees all men as 'fearful of being alone and needing a good woman to take care of them'—as if she can bribe someone into marrying her!"

There's no end to the diversity of Projections that you may find.

Next, ask yourself how each person in your life sees you. Is anyone far afield? If so, trouble may be brewing. But using the Projection Principle, you can stop playing into the Projection and start changing it.

Human nature will doubtless never enable you or those closest to you to achieve pure objectivity. But now at least you can take a major step in that direction.